HUMMER H3™

Larry Edsall

MOTORBOOKS

On the front cover: The HUMMER H3 offers the design cues and off-road capabilities that have made the HUMMER H1 and H2 so popular, but it puts them in a much more affordable and accessible package. *Jim Fets*

On the frontispiece: A HUMMER H3 prototype makes a big splash on a rain-soaked trail in Arizona's red rock country. *Brenda Priddy & Company*

On the title page: A HUMMER family photo includes staff, designers, engineers, and their vehicles (from left) the H3, H2 SUT, H1 wagon, H1 open-top, H2, and another H3.

On the back cover: The HUMMER H3 leads the H2 and H1 over a slick rock trail.

On the back cover (inset): The HUMMER H3 is king of the mountain among mid-sized sport utility vehicles.

ISBN-13: 978-0-7603-2195-9
ISBN-10: 0-7603-2195-7

Editor: Lindsay Hitch
Designer: GGS

Printed in China

Contents

Dedication

For Mom, who went against the advice of friends and family—"He'll poke his eyes out!"—to let her toddler son play with pencil and paper. She showed her son how to form the letters and words that would be the building blocks for his future.

Acknowledgments

I have many people to thank for making this book possible, including my seventh- and eighth-grade English teacher, Mrs. Ward, who made me diagram all those sentences and, in the process, taught me to appreciate the wonderful way our language works.

I also thank Tom Kowaleski, Peter Ternes, and especially David Caldwell and Dayna Hart of the General Motors public relations staff for opening doors and providing access to HUMMER executives, product planners, designers, and engineers. I assure you this book could not have been written without Dayna's patience with me and her persistence in finding folks to answer my questions and to share their photos.

Among those who answered those questions were Mike DiGiovanni, Susan Docherty, Roger McCormack, Marc Hernandez, and Michele Mack, as well as Clay Dean, Holt Ware, and Jon Albert from design staff, and engineers Tom Wallace, Brooks Stover, Lori Cumming, Kevin Dinger, Todd Hubbard, Jenna Pechauer, and Rob Fritsch. Dinger

and Hubbard deserve special mention; they took the risk of riding along when I was at the wheel.

Craig Mac Nab and Lee Woodward gave me insight into HUMMER heritage during a visit to South Bend.

At Shreveport, where the H3 is built, plant public relations coordinator Donna McLallen was my tour guide and provided introductions to David Gibbons, Ryal Siem, Doug Kast, Patrick Bloom, Gaye McCarty, Jim Graham, Tammy Armstrong, Betsy Burke, Susana Escudero, Dawn Williams, and many others, including Marilyn Allen, human resources development representative for UAW Local 2166, who made photographer Neil Johnson's work much easier. Johnson, who has a studio in Shreveport, was one of two professional photographers who were part of this project. The other was Brenda Priddy, the acclaimed automotive spy photographer who chronicled a day of off-roading in an H3 prototype in Arizona.

Others who provided photography, including the images from the design and engineering departments and all of the shots of the development drives in places such as the Rubicon and Moab, include Kevin MacFadden, Kevin Dinger, Daryl Erlich, Lisa Yamin, Todd Hubbard, Dayna Hart, Wayne Morrical, and David Cubitt of GM. Additional images came from Chris Jensen and Cathy Powell of Modernista!, Bill Isenberg of Iconix and some early Jeep vehicle images were shared by the DaimlerChrysler archives.

Others who were more than helpful include John Chapman and David Williams of GM's Desert Proving Grounds; the folks at Capitol HUMMER of Lansing, Michigan, for the tour of their new store; David Stewart of Bridgestone; and Joe Kovach, my former coworker at *AutoWeek* magazine.

Those at MBI Publishing Company who had direct hands in this project include Zack Miller, Lee Klancher, Leah Cochenet Noel, and Lindsay Hitch, as well as content editor Kris Palmer and proofreader Janice Cauley. I need to thank Zack Miller and Lee Klancher for their persistence regarding this project. I had just finished my most recent book, on the history, design, and development of the Ford GT, and was at Book Expo America (the annual trade show of book publishers and booksellers), where, over dinner, Zack, Lee, and I talked about potential subjects for my next project for MBI

Publishing Company. I had several ideas to suggest. They wanted to do a book like the one on GT about the HUMMER H3.

"I hate Hummers," I responded, telling them about how impractical and even embarrassing it had been to do a test drive of an H1 in an urban environment. I admitted that the H2 was a much more practical vehicle for civilian duties, but I had a whole list of other book projects I was eager to undertake.

"But we really like the GT book and that format and we want you to do the same thing on the H3," they insisted. They wouldn't take no for an answer, and now I'm glad they didn't give in.

Sure, I'd still like to turn those other projects into published books. But had I not undertaken this one, I would have missed what I hope you'll find to be a fascinating story and the tale of a vehicle development program that changed a lot of thinking at General Motors. I wouldn't have met folks such as Craig Mac Nab or Mickey D or Holt Ware or Susan Docherty. I wouldn't have had my own epiphany about the essence of HUMMER, how a vehicle can be real and responsible—and still do the Rubicon.

You see, the HUMMER H3 really is a vehicle for change.

Like Nothing Else
The Essence of HUMMER

THE QUESTION IS NOT WHO CAN KEEP UP WITH HUMMER...

THE QUESTION IS WHO CAN FOLLOW?

Though HUMMERs are known more for strength than for speed, veteran off-road racer Rod Hall's team has competed in HUMMERs since 1993. An H1 driven by Hall's son Chad and Roger Norman won the Full Stock production class in the grueling Baja 1000 in 2001.

ALL ACCESS—or ALL AXIS—either one could serve as the official vanity plate for the new HUMMER H3. That's because this "unlike anything else" vehicle can conquer the kind of angles and obstacles that would stop most others in their tracks. Like its big brothers the HUMMER H1 and HUMMER H2, the HUMMER H3 not only looks like nothing else on—or off—the road, but it can also go (and perhaps even more importantly, return from) places where ordinary vehicles and their ordinary drivers fear to tread.

Yes, with the HUMMER H3, the HUMMER brand continues to be far from ordinary, building on its no-compromise, complete-the-mission reputation. But the H3's mission is slightly different from its siblings'. It has the iconic styling and unmatched off-road capability of the HUMMER brand, but has also been made more accessible—more accessible to more people and to even more places.

After all, there are places where the H1 and H2 can't go. Those vehicles are simply too big for some narrow off-road trails. They sometimes don't fit in urban parking places or some family garages. They also don't always fit into family budgets. But with a base price less than $30,000, and with a fuel-economy rating of up to 20 miles per gallon, the HUMMER H3 is made more for real people, not just the pro athletes, rap stars, and movie celebrities that helped make the HUMMER brand as popular as it is.

Yes, most of us know the HUMMER because of people like Arnold Schwarzenegger, General Norman Schwarzkopf, and the coalition troops of Desert Storm. But it was the behind-the-scenes people, like AM General's CEO Jim Armour and those at General Motors that really brought the HUMMER ideal to life. These people, such as Mike DiGiovanni, Clay Dean, and so many others, had an epiphany for what HUMMER should be. Once they discovered the vehicle's essence—what it is and must be—they wouldn't back down from that ideal. Just like the vehicle they created, these people were on a mission and would not take "no" for an answer.

Because of their drive, the HUMMER, and especially its H3 incarnation, became a vehicle for change—a vehicle that spurred a change in the way the world's largest automaker does business; a vehicle that will prompt other car manufacturers to consider how they develop new concepts. Through the H2, H3, and eventually the H4 and more, General Motors realizes that it no longer can simply take one of its basic vehicles, make a few cosmetic changes, and call it something else. Too often in the past, GM, as well as other automakers and auto buyers, have been willing to accept "good enough."

Remember when GM sold a Chevrolet Citation as a Cadillac Cimarron? Or more recently, when GM tried to do the same thing by importing an Opel Omega and rebadging it as the Cadillac Catera? Such moves eventually cost GM billions of dollars as it had to rebuild the Cadillac's image and its product line. Now, the renaissance of GM's luxury marque is one of the biggest automotive success stories of the turn of the twenty-first century—the sort of comeback market research gurus do case studies about in business school.

When GM contracted to take on the HUMMER brand, it faced an old temptation—to take a Chevrolet Tahoe, make as few modifications as possible, and offer it up as the HUMMER H2. Or, take the Chevrolet Colorado, give it the profile of a HUMMER-like sport utility vehicle, bolt on some larger wheels and tires, and call it the H3. But that didn't happen. It wasn't allowed to happen. That wasn't good enough.

Like the H2, the H3 is no mere carryover vehicle. It is a new vehicle, one designed and engineered to be a HUMMER, a real HUMMER, which is not to be confused with a real Humvee. The H3 is not a war wagon; it is a premium vehicle that can carry you not just down the road but also up and over the Rubicon Trail.

Sure, a HUMMER may have some parts and pieces and general undercarriage architecture that are carried over from a Tahoe or Colorado, but not nearly as many as you might expect—nor nearly as many as some at GM had hoped. Instead, people such as Mike DiGiovanni, former HUMMER general manager, Susan Docherty, who succeeded DiGiovanni as general manager in the summer of 2004, and the others on the HUMMER team refused to deviate from the essence of what HUMMER is.

Author Larry Edsall takes a turn at the wheel of a HUMMER H3 prototype during a test drive near Sedona, Arizona. **Brenda Priddy & Company**

And what is that essence? Over and over and over again, I've heard the same thing from everyone involved in making this brand: HUMMER's essence is its iconic design teamed with its unparalleled ability to deal with unpaved terrain. When you see a HUMMER, you're not going to confuse it with anything else on the road or trail. And when you drive a HUMMER, you're going to drive with the confidence that you're able to go just about anywhere you would need or want to go.

These characteristics were present in the first Humvees, giving them the right stuff for demanding military operations. Then, these features carried over to the first civilian HUMMERs, the H1 and the H2. And now they live on in the H3. Because without these defining features, the newest General Motors brand might not succeed, might not live on to the future. The H1, H2, H3, or H4 and more must all be like each other—and therefore they must be "like nothing else."

Chapter 1

General Agreement

How Humvee became HUMMER

"You guys are nuts if you don't do this!"

—*Arnold Schwarzenegger*

The HUMMER H3 has a strong stance and powerful presence from seemingly every angle.

January 17, 1991—dinner is delayed by live television coverage of the bombing of Baghdad. Then, a few days later, American and coalition armed forces undertake the largest invasion since World War II, rolling across the Kuwaiti desert in vehicles that look like sand-colored Jeeps but are much larger, vehicles that look like rolling bunkers, carrying soldiers and a variety of large and serious weaponry.

From that day forward, these vehicles would represent the fight for freedom, the fight against tyranny. Officially, they are the American military's High-Mobility Multipurpose Wheeled Vehicles—known as HMMWVs in Pentagon procurement speak, but pronounced "Humvee" by the soldiers who depend on them.

Their predecessors—spare, rugged, sure-footed Jeeps—are now nearly 20 years out of date, vehicles that in the post-Vietnam era are not equipped to carry the modern military's increasing payloads. However, the small and nimble Jeeps have made a smooth transition into civilian life, becoming popular among those who love the vehicle's off-road capabilities, the access Jeeps give to wide-open spaces and narrow, muddy trails.

On alert: American soldiers go through training with their Humvees. **AM General**

AM General traces its roots to Willys-Overland, which produced Jeeps for American troops throughout World War II. Note: The hood ornament was not standard issue. **DaimlerChrysler archives**

To replace them, the military started looking in the late 1970s for a vehicle to carry troops into combat zones but versatile enough to serve as a remote communications station or platform for a rocket launcher. The military needed the vehicles to be compact enough to fit into the hold of a cargo plane, but tough enough to be shoved out the back of that plane or dropped from a tow-hook beneath a helicopter. The vehicle also had to be fast enough to keep pace with the new M1 Abrams tanks and Bradley fighting vehicles. It had to have the power and dexterity to deal with terrain—urban or desert, mountain or snowfield—that would turn back any multipurpose wheeled vehicle currently on the market.

When drafting these requirements into specifications, the defense department asked for the following:

- The HMMWV needed to travel at 60 miles per hour (and at 30 miles per hour with flat tires).
- It would have a range of at least 300 miles between refueling stops.
- It would climb a 60 percent grade and traverse a 40 percent side grade.
- It would turn a circle within 25 feet and ford a 30-inch-deep stream.
- It would protect its occupants from a 16-gram fragment hitting at 225 meters per second.

The M1025A2 is built in various configurations, including this armament/tow missile carrier configuration. A Humvee can ford 30 inches of water, or 60 inches when equipped with a snorkel unit. AM General

To meet military specifications, a HMMWV has to be able to climb a 60 percent grade. AM General

Equipped with tires 37 inches tall, a HMMWV can tackle all sorts of abusive environments. A central tire inflation system (CTIS) enables the driver to adjust air pressure for enhanced traction in such challenging terrain as deep mud or soft sand. AM General

Where There's a Willys, There's a Way

AM GENERAL'S ROOTS GO BACK TO 1903, with its oldest ancestral vehicle being the 1903 Overland Runabout automobile. Overland ran into financial trouble early, though, and had to be rescued by its biggest customer, auto dealer John North Willys. Willys was determined to bring the company back from the brink, even if it meant building cars in a big circus tent for a year. By 1912, Willys was producing four Overland models in a large factory in Toledo, Ohio. Willys' cars were so popular that for a period of several years, only Henry Ford's company was selling more vehicles.

Willys was so successful that in 1917 he merged his company with aircraft maker Curtiss. The merger took Willys back East, away from the daily Toledo operation, and Willys-Overland suffered his absence. He eventually returned, got the company back on its feet, only to have the Great Depression put it back in dire straights.

Yet again, Willys rallied the company, though the effort took its toll and he died of heart attack in the spring of 1935. Nonetheless, in 1940 the company was sound enough to win an army contract to build a quarter-ton, four-wheel-drive, general-purpose vehicle designed by American Bantam—the ancestor of the very Jeep AM General's HMMWV later would replace.

After World War II, Willys-Overland retained rights to produce Jeeps for civilians and later to build military versions for use in the Korean War. Soon after that conflict, shipbuilder and construction magnate Henry J. Kaiser's automaker, Kaiser-Frazer, bought out Willys-Overland. Then, in the mid-1960s, the newest incarnation of Willys-Overland, now known as Kaiser Jeep Corporation, bought a Studebaker plant in South Bend, Indiana, and converted it to build 5-ton military trucks.

"A little team was sent to South Bend and took over the contract and the plant," says AM General spokesman Craig Mac Nab. "That's us. That's where we come from."

In 1970, American Motors acquired the former Kaiser Jeep and the company's defense and government products division became known as AM General. This branch operated out of an old automotive bumper plant east of Mishawaka, Indiana—the plant that would later become the home of the Humvee. Faced with its own financial problems, American Motors sold AM General to LTV Corporation— a conglomerate encompassing businesses involved in steel making, aerospace, and defense. But LTV had problems of its own. "For most of the time we belonged to them, they were in Chapter 11 because of pension problems in their steel business," Mac Nab says.

Despite such financial woes, AM General placed its bid when the Pentagon sought a replacement for the Jeep and very soon its HUMMER would be known around the world.

From all of the manufacturers' various creations, the military selected only three vehicles for final trials. During the trials, these vehicles went through more than 600,000 miles of testing, including evaluation in several simulated combat environments and terrains from around the globe. Then, on March 22, 1983, the U.S. Army Tank Automotive & Armaments Command signed a $1.2 billion contract with the AM General Division of LTV Aerospace and Defense to produce 55,000 High-Mobility Multipurpose Wheeled Vehicles (HMMWVs), in 15 different configurations, over a five-year period.

The question was, could AM General produce these vehicles? The company had a long, if not irregular, history of financial challenges, yet it had persevered through them all.

While the Humvee that AM General developed was well received, AM General didn't even submit a bid in 1988 when the U.S. Army was letting a contract to build a new medium-duty truck. With parent company LTV Corporation under a $7 billion debt load, there wasn't enough money to expand production.

"We were doomed," Craig Mac Nab, spokesman for AM General, remembers. "Humvee was really all we had going and it didn't look like there was going to be another Humvee contract."

Luckily, the AM General's long string of rebounds was not at an end. The next year, the military ordered

This 1940 model was one of the first "quads" produced by Willys-Overland Motors. **DaimlerChrysler archives**

another 33,000 HMMWVs—from the only company geared to produce them. Then Saddam Hussein started firing Scud missiles and the prospect of Humvee production drying up suddenly became remote.

WHILE REAL SOLDIERS TOOK EVERY ADVANTAGE of the Humvee's capabilities, another man of action was about to influence the vehicle's future—movie megastar Arnold Schwarzenegger. During the shooting of his 1990 film, *Kindergarten Cop*, in Oregon, Schwarzenegger saw a Humvee coming down the road. "That's really cool," he thought. "I'd like that vehicle."

Yet the vehicle Schwarzenegger wanted—a civilian version of the Humvee—did not yet exist. Of course, that didn't stop The Terminator from trying to get one. He

had read about the Humvee before—two of them had competed in a rally from London to Beijing.

"We took two Humvees and made them into something that looks something like the wagon we make now," Mac Nab says of those early civilian-type Humvees, adding that AM General's CEO Jim Armour saw a small but viable market in a civilian version of the Humvee and used the rally to see how such a vehicle might perform.

So when Schwarzenegger contacted AM General about buying a Humvee of his own, the company did have to think about it—but not for long. "Here's a guy who at the time had the highest Q [celebrity credibility] rating, was the biggest movie star in the world, and he

wants to drive one of our vehicles," Mac Nab says. "Don't you think we should figure out how to let him?"

In June 1991, Arnold received his one-off civilian Hummer, a converted Humvee, and immediately became friends with AM General's Jim Armour. As they got to know each other better, Schwarzenegger kept telling him that his plans for series production of the civilian HUMMER were a good idea. "You guys are nuts if you don't do this!" he said.

Converting a Humvee into a street-legal vehicle was neither easy nor inexpensive, but AM General decided to try it. The modifications required included converting 24-volt NATO electrical systems to 12-volt setups, meeting federal motor vehicle safety standards, installing a much

After World War II, Jeeps made the transition to civilian life and allowed many people to explore the point where the pavement ends.

DaimlerChrysler archives

The front skid plate on the HUMMER H2 was engineered to protect components from damage in severe off-roading, but it was designed with aesthetics in mind and proudly displays the vehicle's logo.

more civilized interior with roll-up windows and some padding, and painting them in something other than the flat sand color specified in the military contract.

Even with those changes, the very first $100,000 civilian HUMMERs were overbuilt, even for the most rugged of sport utility vehicles. A civilian vehicle didn't need bumpers that were strong enough to keep it tethered to a helicopter. Yet civilians wanted them: AM General was selling as many as 1,000 HUMMERs a year. "We sold the first ones by mail," Mac Nab says. "There was an 800 number you could call and we'd mail you a packet that had a videotape and an order form and a brochure that unfolded into a poster."

Company CEO Jim Armour knew that even more people would want these HUMMERs if they were smaller and less expensive. But to make that a reality, AM would need the help of another General—General Motors.

IN JANUARY 1999, MIKE DIGIOVANNI, head of General Motors' Market Intelligence Group, presented the automaker's North American Strategy Board with what he considered to be a trio of blockbuster ideas. One was rejected by Ron Zarella, then president of GM's North American Operations, as the "stupidest" thing he'd ever heard; another, Zarella called "over the top." Finally,

DiGiovanni's last blockbuster won favor: General Motors should purchase the HUMMER brand and develop a portfolio of HUMMER vehicles.

"Why don't you go down to AM General and see if they're interested," Zarella suggested. DiGiovanni decided to take along enough GM brass to show he was serious, including new general manager of the Chevrolet brand, Kurt Ritter; North American Operations CFO Paul Schmidt; and Jack Hazen of the GM finance department.

At AM General, the GM contingent met Armour, who said he and his staff had been thinking about building a vehicle that was smaller and more nimble than the original HUMMER. He also was tired of the way DaimlerChrysler's Jeep brand had been bragging about its leadership in off-road capability. He was sure a new HUMMER would demonstrate that even Jeep had some things to learn about off-roading.

As the negotiations progressed, the GM representatives noted that they were only interested in buying the HUMMER brand, not taking over AM General completely. They also seemed to accept that a true civilian HUMMER had to be more than a rebadged GM vehicle.

After the visit, the companies continued to talk. Months later, as the year was coming to an end, they reached a formal agreement. It spelled out that GM would lend AM General the money to build a new

Like the H2, the HUMMER H2 SUT is built at the assembly facility near Mishawaka, Indiana. The H3 is built in a GM factory in Shreveport, Louisiana, and is the only HUMMER with a home outside northern Indiana.
AM General

Michael DiGiovanni pushed hard to get a job at General Motors. Once there, he pushed the company to pursue the HUMMER brand and then served as the first general manager of GM's newest division.

assembly plant to produce the new HUMMER. In return, AM General would pay back that loan through the manufacturing fee it earned for each vehicle it built. Finally, GM would own the rights to the HUMMER brand, would establish a network of HUMMER dealerships to sell the vehicle, and in the future could design and produce more new HUMMER vehicles.

The job to make all of the above happen fell to Mike DiGiovanni, and it would take every bit of persistence he could muster. Fortunately, he knew how to be persistent. DiGiovanni grew up in Detroit and the only job he ever really wanted was one inside the GM headquarters building. After earning a graduate degree in economics, he sent his resume time and again to the automaker—for 10 years. After a while, he got this

response in a letter: "We do not want to hear from you again." Yet he refused to take no for an answer, not the first time he would do so with GM.

He finally got his foot in the door at General Motors in 1979, when he was hired into a new division that would deal with rail, road, and water freight delivery. Unfortunately, only a month after he was hired, the second oil shock of the decade struck and the new division was quickly disassembled. DiGiovanni found refuge on the GM economics staff. By 1997 he was in charge of market research and forecasting, where he identified market phenomena before they blossomed into trends.

One of those buds was the public's interest in sport utility vehicles with rugged, militaristic styling and

The product of a joint venture involving engineers from AM General and General Motors, the HUMMER H2 displays amazing off-road prowess.

extreme off-road capabilities. In DiGiovanni's research, he found that potential customers wanted these vehicles to perform as well as they looked. Fortunately, Tom Davis, head of GM truck programs, knew that was important too. They arranged an off-road test drive to see what gulf separated GM's 4x4s from AM General's Hummer. With

its new Tahoe in development, GM engineers brought that along for the drive, as well as GM four-wheel-drive pickup trucks.

"[The AM General people] were honestly impressed by the mobility of our products," says Ken Lindensmith,

continued on page 28

DESIGN ACTIONABLES
- EXREMELY CAPABLE
- BRUTAL
- OVERBUILT

POSITIONING

REASON FOR BEING	TARGET
-MAINTAIN HUMMER AS THE PREMIER OFF-ROAD VEHICLE & MOST EXCLUSIVE ASPIRATIONAL BRAND	-RUGGED
	-SUCCESS
	-EXTREME
-BUILD ON HUMMER'S CELEBRITY STATUS & WORLD-RENOWNED REPUTATION EARNED IN COMBAT	-FERVENT

"Brand positioning" statements for the design and development of the HUMMER H2 show how the original HMMWV was used to provide inspiration for the more civilized vehicles that would follow.

DESIGN TACTICS

OVERALL PROPORTIONS & ATTRIBUTES
- High ground clearance
- Wheels at the corners
- Huge wheels and tires
- Flat glass
- Thin window openings

ET	DIFFERENTIATED BENEFIT
⌐UAL	-Combat capable
⌐IEVER	-Exclusive
	-Brutal
⌐ADER	-Overbuilt

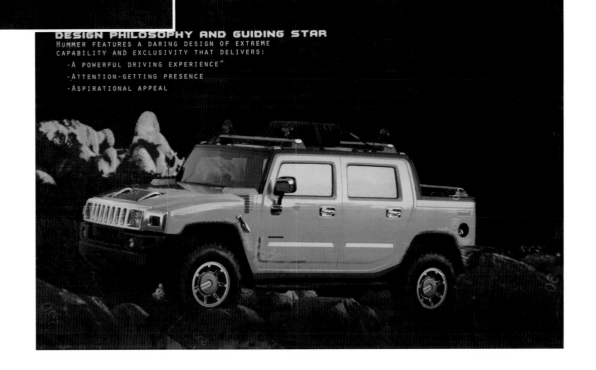

DESIGN PHILOSOPHY AND GUIDING STAR
Hummer features a daring design of extreme capability and exclusivity that delivers:
- A powerful driving experience"
- Attention-getting presence
- Aspirational appeal

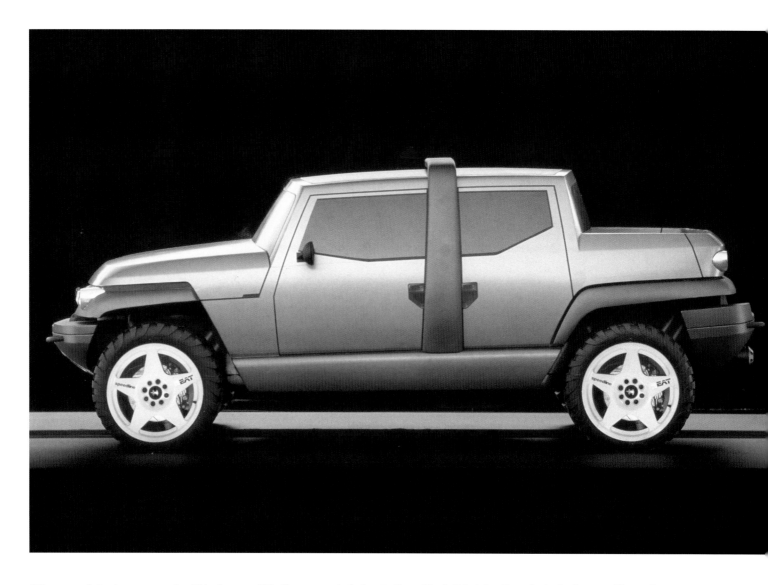

GM was ready to show a concept vehicle, known within the company's design studio as Chunk II, but the Chevrolet-badged sport utility project was put on hold after the company acquired the rights to the HUMMER brand.

Continued from page 25
who later would lead GM's HUMMER H2 development team. Still, he admits that that first run was more than a little rough. "We got through all the obstacles, it was just rather painful."

"At the end of the day, our trucks were dirty and theirs were damaged," AM General's Craig Mac Nab adds.

—————————

WORK ALREADY WAS WELL ADVANCED IN THE SUMMER OF 1999 IN THE GM DESIGN STUDIO on a new sport utility vehicle concept that had very aggressive lines.

Nicknamed Chunk II, it was slated to be featured at the North American International Auto Show in January 2000 and badged as a Chevrolet.

"We had a concept vehicle that was virtually done—this was July of '99—and Wayne Cherry [GM vice president of design] came into my office. He shut the door and said, 'I want you to work on a vehicle at home,'" Clay Dean, chief designer in GM's truck brand center, recalls.

Cherry revealed that GM was in negotiation with AM General and wanted to have a concept vehicle ready for the Detroit show, one that would establish the design

cues for a second HUMMER, an H2, that would be sold by a new network of GM-franchised dealers. Cherry said Dean could not discuss the project, not even with his own studio team. During the day, he had to work just as hard as ever on Chunk II, even though that concept might never be seen outside the studio. At night, his attentions would go to HUMMER.

Dean was surprised at how quickly his sketches took shape. He drew on the Humvee to establish what would become HUMMER's iconic design cues: an upright windshield, planer (flat) lines, a long dash-to-axle ratio (the front axle set well ahead of the dashboard), high sills and beltline, turret-style windows, large wheels pushed to the corners, a cabin cradled between the axles, short front and rear overhangs, and lots of ground clearance.

Dean's work was so secret that after he was done sketching at home, Cherry had a separate and clandestine studio set up for him to take his work from sketches to clay models and a full-scale concept vehicle. They had a clay model finished by the end of September, yet even at that point, there was no official HUMMER division of General Motors. So instead of being assigned a typical alphanumeric development program name, the work inside the secret studio was known only as "Project Maria"—codenamed after Arnold Schwarzenegger's wife, Kennedy clan member and television journalist, Maria Schriver.

Months later, the whole world found out about Project Maria when a steel-bodied, running concept vehicle was unveiled on January 2, 2000, at the big Detroit auto show.

Not that it's likely, but just in case someone isn't sure just what the H2 might be, letters in the center of its grille bars emphasize that this vehicle is, indeed, a HUMMER.

The shift lever that looks like it came straight from a jet airplane's cockpit served as the signature element in an H2 interior that features a full array of gauges, well-bolstered seats, and other upscale appointments.

DESIGNING A HUMMER-INSPIRED H2 concept vehicle was one thing; developing a production vehicle that would live up to a HUMMER badge turned out to be quite another.

"We had to go figure out how to really do that. Can we really do that?" DiGiovanni says. "We didn't know if we could."

Neither did anyone else.

"A lot of people were skeptical that it wouldn't be an authentic HUMMER, that it would be a rebadged Tahoe," he says. "The *Wall Street Journal* had an article saying that's probably what it would be. People were all skeptical, so we really worked hard to be an authentic HUMMER, to be the premier off-road vehicle."

While the H2 Vision Vehicle was touring the auto show circuit, creating interest in the promised production version of the vehicle, engineers from GM, AM General, and supplier consultants went to work to figure out how to fulfill that promise.

"We knew we would be scrutinized by everybody," DiGiovanni says, so much of the development money went into making sure the vehicle had a particularly rugged chassis underneath it. "We figured that if it wasn't [premiere off-road], the brand would never survive. It had to be the best, not just best-in-class, but the best off-road vehicle bar none, except for the H1."

When it comes to off-road capability, the gap between HUMMER H1s and everything else is huge, adds

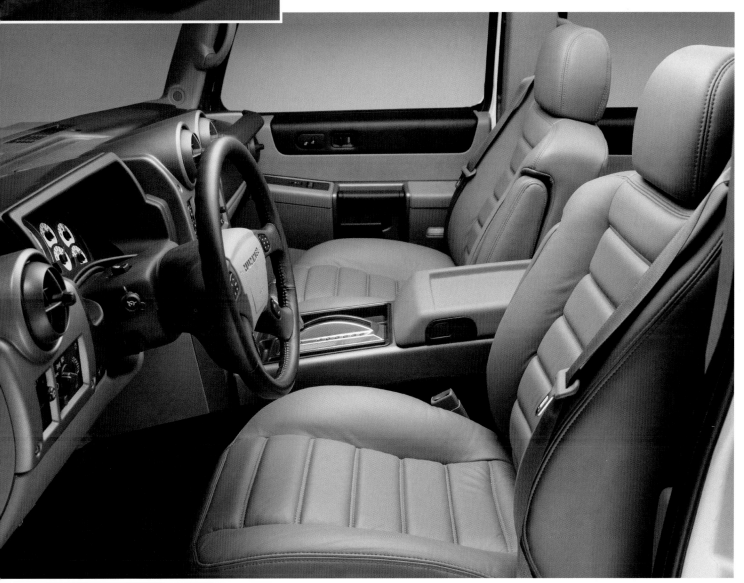

AM General's spokesman Mac Nab. "It really isn't fair to compare it to anything else," he says. "We used to have a slogan that I still love: 'It's not whether anybody else can keep up; it's whether anybody can follow.' Since the gulf between the H1 and everything else was so huge, there was plenty of room for the H2 to be better than anything else except the H1."

The development team anticipated that perhaps half of the components that would go into the H2 could come from GM's new GMT800 pickup trucks and sport utility vehicles. But when decisions had to be made between the existing parts and the development of new ones that would provide HUMMER-caliber off-road capabilities, the decision was to stay true to the mission of off-road supremacy. As a result, when the H2 was launched in 2002 as a 2003 model, many of the parts that had been carried from GM's 800-series vehicles were extensively modified and strengthened.

The work paid off: HUMMER H2 became a big hit, both for its design and its dynamic capabilities. "This H2 is everything the current HUMMER is: big enough, plenty beefy, powerful, and unique," *4-Wheel & Off-Road* magazine touted. "However, the H2 is also everything the old HUMMER isn't: it's less expensive, smaller, quieter, more comfortable, and highly stylish, and it performs great."

AutoWeek added: "We crept, crawled, and connived a caravan of [H2s] over Moab's infamous Poison Spider and Golden Spike trails, two of the hardest four-wheel-drive routes on the planet. Real four-wheeling like this is fun. . . . This here HUMMER H2's the best dang four-by ever made."

Mission accomplished. Well, at least the first one.

Like a child maneuvering a giant Tonka toy through a sandbox, the H2 driver finds pleasure in playtime.

Chapter 2

The Trick Truck

Diversionary Tactics

"Let's see if we can cause a little bit of puckering if we come out with a pickup truck."

—Marc Hernandez, HUMMER product director

Although the H3 was well along in its development as a sport utility vehicle, HUMMER decided to produce the H3T concept vehicle as a two-door pickup truck, in part to throw a curveball to competitors, in part to see how consumers would react to a compact pickup with HUMMER qualities.

Anyone who anticipated that the HUMMER lineup would stop at the H1 and "son of HUMMER" H2 (and perhaps variants such as the H2 SUT, with its small pickup truck bed) didn't understand the economics of building an automotive brand.

To create and sustain a viable dealership network and to keep factories running, an automaker has to maintain a steady stream and variety of vehicles. Sure, an exotic sports car maker such as Ferrari might get by with just a couple of very expensive models, but even Porsche offers four series, including a sport utility, with several variations of each vehicle.

From the moment it pursued the HUMMER brand, General Motors knew that an H3 would become the volume vehicle.

H1 was selling in the hundreds of units each year. Even with a new assembly line at the AM General plant in Mishawaka, Indiana, H2 would have annual production capacity of only 40,000 units. And sales would be limited by a sticker price in the mid-$50,000 range.

General Motors figured that H3 could dramatically increase accessibility to the HUMMER brand. It would be a smaller vehicle, and would be developed with a considerably lower base price target, albeit one within the premium end of the automotive marketplace. It would be built in one of GM's own plants, allowing for greatly increased capacity.

H3 also would be designed and developed to serve as someone's primary daily driver, not as a very expensive toy like the H1, or as a second or third member of a family fleet like the H2. Unlike the H1 and H2, fuel economy would be a consideration, with a 20-mile-per-gallon highway rating as one of the development targets.

"The H3 was planned all along," says Mike DiGiovanni, who served as general manager of the HUMMER brand from its creation until the summer of 2004, when he was promoted to executive director of GM's North American sales, service, and marketing.

While it was important for H2 to follow H1 to establish the HUMMER brand and its image, "the H3 had to happen for dealers to justify their investment," DiGiovanni adds.

And it was a big investment. HUMMER would be a premium brand, not another mainstream marque, and GM expected each of the anticipated 170 or more HUMMER dealers across the country to build a new and specially designed Quonset-hut-style showroom complex with an adjacent rock-crawling, water-fording, side-hill-sloping, angle-of-approach-and-departure-challenging "capabilities demonstration area," where every Hummer's unparalleled off-road capabilities could be experienced in a way that no test drive around the block could duplicate.

"Everyone had to swallow hard," says DiGiovanni. "It's not easy to invest millions of dollars." And it wasn't only the dealers to whom that applied. Before dealers could sell an H3, General Motors had to build one, and just as with the H2, there would be considerable pressure within GM for the H3 to use as many existing components as possible.

For the H3, those components would come from the GMT355—the new midsize pickup truck that GM had under development for Chevrolet and GMC. A sport utility vehicle (SUV) was part of the GMT355's product prospectus from the very beginning. But back in the mid-1990s when the program was approved, there was no expectation that the SUV would be anything other than a standard Chevrolet/GMC vehicle designed to succeed the Blazer/Jimmy, just as the 355 (Chevrolet Colorado/GMC Canyon) would replace the S-10/Sonoma. No one anticipated that a 355-based SUV would have to be tough enough to be a HUMMER.

When GM acquired the HUMMER brand late in 1999, the first priority was to get to work on H2. But almost immediately, the design studio was sketching ideas for a potential H3. Preliminary engineering was

Urban bivouac was the design theme for the unique HUMMER dealership architecture, which was patterned on the military Quonset hut. Pavlik Design of Fort Lauderdale, Florida, created the unique dealership architecture.

underway by the fall of 2000.

Officially, the HUMMER H3 was approved as production program GMT345 on October 31, 2002. GM kept the decision quiet, however, because it had made no announcement yet that it would produce a HUMMER beyond the H2.

"We did do something a little unusual," says Brooks Stover, vehicle line (day-to-day engineering) director for the HUMMER H3. Very early in the design process, "we created a logo. The design guys did a red shield that looks like a military patch that the Third Brigade would have on its uniform shoulders. It has a lightning stripe, and it's red and yellow and looks real military, and it says 345. We used that on a lot of [internal] documents because we couldn't say 'H3.'"

ONE OF THOSE DOCUMENTS WAS THE "GMT345 VOICE OF DESIGN," issued December 18, 2000, to lay out H3 design parameters, which included high ground clearance, short overhangs, an upright windshield, long dash-to-axle ratio, a high beltline, a cabin cradled between the axles, a wider-than-tall stance, and

innovative styling. In addition to the HUMMER's iconic design cues, the H3 would include such style innovations as a full-width sunroof, wash-out interior, and removable fenders for extreme off-roading.

As it became obvious that an H3 was in development, the company prepared an H3-inspired concept vehicle. To tempt the vehicle-buying public and misdirect GM's competitors, the H3T went onto the auto show circuit early in 2004.

"We were very far along on the H3 when we started to develop the H3T concept," says Clay Dean, the H2 designer who had become chief of the HUMMER

brand character studio, a design think tank for the new brand. "We wanted to do a vehicle that showed what the theme was going to be, but in a different configuration, because up to this point, all anybody had thought a HUMMER could be was an SUV. We wanted to say, 'No, it can be a lot of things.' It could be a little small pickup truck. So we did a pickup derivative, which is having a lot of internal influence on other vehicles that could come out of the HUMMER portfolio.

"All the cues and all the visuals are from the H3, though with even further refinement," continues Dean. "Was the H3T a misdirection? Sure it was. The reason for

doing a concept vehicle, a lot of it, is to gauge consumer reaction: How do you feel about this?"

The H3T was unveiled at the 2004 Los Angeles Auto Show. This was like no HUMMER anyone had seen before. It was a midsize pickup truck that certainly had HUMMER design cues, but that looked even smaller than it was because of its architectural proportions.

"There was a lot of speculation by a lot of folks, some of them our competitors, about what we were going to come out with in the H3," says Marc Hernandez, product director for the HUMMER brand. "We thought, 'Let's see how the market reacts to the pickup, what our competitors do. Let's see if we can cause a little bit of puckering if we come out with a pickup truck.'"

This sketch of the HUMMER H3T concept vehicle underscores the military aspect of its inspiration.

A foam model was prepared to accompany the "Voice of Design" document and shows the early expectation that the H3 would be closer to the H1 in its design cues.

Enjoying what he calls "gamesmanship," Hernandez adds, "We had most of the automotive world believing that we were coming out with a midsize pickup!"

"There is no reason for the HUMMER brand to replicate what GMC is doing and what Chevrolet is doing," says Dean. "It is important to us to have a stronger positioning in the marketplace, and it doesn't mean chasing Jeep, and it doesn't mean chasing Range Rover or Toyota or any of the other brands. We think that we need to lead where we need to go."

And don't be surprised if, just as the H2 SUT followed the H2, some sort of H3 SUT is the next vehicle to join the HUMMER lineup.

"Even though there's an H1 pickup truck [and an H2 SUT has just been launched], you really don't see a

lot of them," Dean explains of the thinking behind the H3T concept. "Nor do you see a lot of regular-cab pickups of any kind. The market is moving to extended cabs and crew cabs almost exclusively.

"We said, 'You know, a really nice, simple, straightforward regular-cab truck with a sporting influence, wouldn't that be a great idea? Wouldn't that be a simple back-to-basics story that HUMMER would be known for? Let's do a concept to see what people think, and while we're doing that, let's show them where the H3 is going to be.'"

Yes, he says, H3T may have been misdirection. But, Dean adds, "I think it was more exciting to have a pickup variant because nobody was expecting that, and we were able to telegraph to folks that, 'Hey, we could be doing a

pickup truck next.' And internally we have pickup concepts that we've created and that are at various levels of progress through the organization."

––––––––––

THE H3T CONCEPT ALSO ALLOWED HUMMER DESIGNERS TO EXPLORE NEW ASPECTS of interior styling and materials. To accelerate that process they invited designers from Nike sporting goods to work with them on the concept.

Thus the H3T's 34-inch-tall BFGoodrich tires have treads patterned like the soles on Nike's All Condition Gear (ACG) trail and hiking shoes, with sand paddles, traction pads, and rubber of various hardness differentiated by color and texture.

The concept's Petrol-colored leather seats have inserts covered with chamois-colored Nike Sphere thermal fabric. The same material was used for the

armrests. Seat stitching and other interior accents were done in a color called Paprika Orange. Nike Epic backpacks were integrated into the seat-back clamshells and were held in place by bungee cords.

The rest of the interior design uses various materials to underscore HUMMER's military heritage. The metal gear selector handle folds flat into the center console. Toggle switches activate various controls. The dashboard display includes an altimeter, compass, and inclinometer. The vehicle is equipped with a portable global positioning system (GPS) navigation system and docking station, as well as a portable MP3 player/radio with its own docking unit.

"HUMMER is a luxury brand," says Dean. "But there is an assumption in the marketplace that luxury is wood and leather, and we even get this from Bob Lutz (GM's vice chairman and product development guru). But on the H3T we said, 'No, there's a different side of luxury.'

The H3T concept utility pickup truck looks almost as if it was sculpted out of a single, solid metallic billet.

General Motors designers worked with their counterparts from Nike on certain aspects of the H3T concept, including the backpacks built into the seat backs, seats covered with thermal material, and the design and color of the truck's tire tread.

"When we look at high-end sporting gear, we see exquisite fabrics that are technical and waterproof, that warm you yet are very thin. We see wonderful alloys that are beautiful in the execution. We see carbon fibers. So when you see the inside of the H3T, we were able to explore all those materials and the people we were talking to, they saw that as luxury. In their minds, they know that paying $5,000 for a mountain bike, that's premium and it's carbon and it's titanium, and it's these wonderful alloys. They think, 'That's awesome.'

"The interior of this truck had all of that, so it helped us progress the philosophy that luxury isn't wood and humidors and buttery, buttery, buttery leathers; it can be something very different, something very much in core with HUMMER values."

This ruggedly refined design theme is prevalent in the H3's exterior as well. The concept vehicle is built with an aluminum exoskeleton that is exposed in the windshield surround and door frames. While the standard-cab architecture restricts storage inside the passenger compartment, the pickup bed has side access doors with fold-down steps that expose built-in toolboxes. The tailgate's hinges are exposed and include cantilevers to provide an unbroken floor more than 4 feet wide. To provide an open atmosphere in the tight interior, the top incorporates a power-operated fabric sunroof and the rear window retracts.

Petrol Blue Metallic paint and satin titanium metallic finishes set off the vehicle's taut and minimalist surfaces and its particularly aggressive stance. Wheels are pushed so far to the corners that flared fenders wrap only over, not around, the tires. The concept vehicle provides 11.5 inches of ground clearance, with an approach angle of 51 degrees and a departure angle of 50 degrees.

The gauge array can show not only such things as fuel level and vehicle speed, but altitude and incline angles of a trail being traveled or traversed.

The "exploded" illustration shows some of the special features designed into the H3T concept vehicle, which is built around a lightweight but strong aluminum exoskeleton.

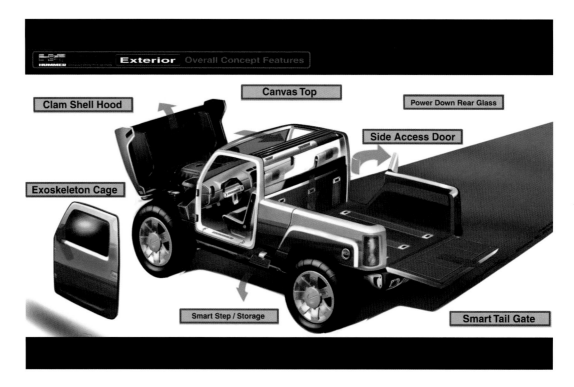

Exterior Overall Concept Features

Clam Shell Hood

Canvas Top

Power Down Rear Glass

Side Access Door

Exoskeleton Cage

Smart Step / Storage

Smart Tail Gate

Access panels and fold-down steps with built-in toolboxes are integrated into the sides of the H3T's truck bed.

Light-emitting diode headlamps illuminate the way ahead while a power-retracting canvas roof (right) provides light and fresh air for the passenger compartment.

Billet or stamped aluminum is used for front and rear brush guards, front and rear axle, and suspension control arm skid plates, the winch cover, and grille surround. Rocker panels are protected by special "rock sliders." A carbon fiber underbody panel serves as a skid plate off-road and to enhance aerodynamics at highway speeds.

The hood pivots forward once trigger-operated latches are released. A forward-facing camera built into the hood louvers for recording off-road excursions.

Designers weren't the only ones having fun with the H3T concept.

While built on a modified midsize truck platform, the H3T concept has locking front and rear axles normally used on full-size trucks. Fifteen-inch Alcon disc brakes have six-piston front and four-piston rear Baer calipers.

Suspension uses Fox remote-reservoir shocks with short/long arm geometry in front and coil-over in the rear.

The automatic four-wheel-drive system draws its power from a heavy-duty Hydra-matic electronically controlled four-speed transmission spun by GM's Vortec 3500 inline five-cylinder engine. The engine is equipped with variable valve timing, variable intake manifold, and two-step variable valve actuation—and for good measure is turbocharged to generate 350 horsepower and 350 ft-lbs of torque.

Concept vehicles create excitement about the brand, but the real test was not whether the HUMMER team could produce a dramatic one-off. The real test was to see if it could design and develop an H3 that would be accepted as a true HUMMER, and could be built, in substantial numbers, in one of GM's own assembly plants.

Here's a concept: Designers built a video camera into the louvers of the H3T hood so off-road adventures could be taped to enjoy again and again.

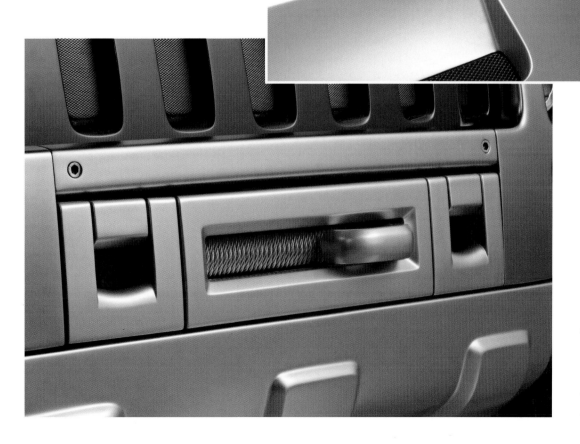

The H3T concept vehicle had a built-in winch, a feature that can be very helpful in serious off-roading. Engineers wanted a similar feature as a factory option on the H3 production vehicle. However, faced with limitations of time, money, and federal crash-test requirements, they were unable to devise one for the start of production.

Chapter 3

Chunk and the Russian Dolls

Evolution of the H3 Design

"We wrung the process out to its fullest."

—Jon Albert, H3 design director

Elements of Chunk's aggressive stance and rakish attitude (above) carried over into Holt Ware's design of the HUMMER H3 (left).

Meet Chunk. Chunk is a General Motors concept vehicle that didn't make it onto the auto show circuit. Except for those invited to focus group research sessions, Chunk has not been seen outside GM—until now.

To accurately tell the story of the design of the HUMMER H3, we have to start with Chunk.

"It looked like a hamburger," says Holt Ware, who can get away with calling Chunk anything he wants because it was Ware who designed Chunk in 1997, and who later would design the HUMMER H3. "The whole thing was very lean and very high.

"It was all up on four wheels. It was all sympathetic to approach and departure [angles]," he continues. But Ware also gave Chunk just enough rake to its stance to take on an attitude, a personality.

Chunk was part of an intense initiative by GM's advanced design staff to explore every facet of the expanding sport utility vehicle market, from micro vehicles to massive ones, with nearly a dozen segments identified in between. (It was out of this same study that a concept vehicle emerged that would find its way into production as the Cadillac SRX.)

Some of the advanced concepts were given mythological names such as Basilisk and Minotaur. Others were named after footwear or watches. Ware's midsized, extreme-capability off-road vehicle was dubbed Salamander, though when it took shape as a foam model it was obvious it should be called Chunk.

Everyone figured that if Chunk ever went into production, it would be as a Chevrolet, and Chevy's bow tie insignia was on the crossbar across Chunk's grille and on its tailgate.

Focus groups liked Chunk. They liked it even more after they saw it sketched as a four-door. They flat-out loved it when they anticipated that it might be a HUMMER.

Holt Ware's early design sketches portrayed the H3 as an entry-level, two-door vehicle with huge tires barely covered by fender flares.

Several architectures were explored for the H3. This is one of Holt Ware's earliest sketches of a four-door sport utility vehicle. After going off on several tangents, the final H3 design found its way back toward this early drawing.

"I was out at a clinic and they said, 'Holt, do a pencil sketch with four doors,'" Ware recalls. "So we did a quick little pencil sketch and they said, 'That's it!' It just took off."

To gauge the essence of a design, auto companies sometimes put names other than their own brands on vehicles being shown to focus groups. GM knew that Chevy didn't carry the same status with off-road enthusiasts as Jeep or even Ford, both of which had much longer and stronger histories in four-wheel-drive vehicles.

"When we put the HUMMER name on it, it went through the roof," says Mike DiGiovanni, who was in charge of GM's Market Intelligence Group, which was conducting focus group and other research into potential new product lines. DiGiovanni suspected one of those yet untapped market niches would be for rugged off-road vehicles with militaristic design cues,

vehicles like the U.S. Army's HMMWV or its close cousin, the civilian HUMMER.

Inspired by Chunk and the overwhelming response to a four-door version, Clay Dean and his GM Truck Brand Center design team went to work on Chunk II, intending that this one would become a full-fledged running concept vehicle to take a prominent place on the Chevrolet stand at the 2000 North American International Auto Show in Detroit.

Like the original Chunk, Chunk II has not been shown in public—until now—because just before its completion, GM acquired rights to the HUMMER brand. Instead of Chunk II, Dean was assigned to design a new concept vehicle, this one with clear HUMMER styling cues. Thus the HUMMER H2 Vision Vehicle rolled onto the GM stand that January in Detroit.

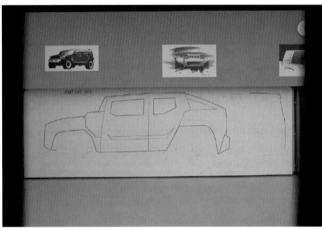

Snapshots taken in the design studio show boards that display the design evolution of the H3, including a full-size outline of an H1-oriented vehicle and a full-size color drawing of one with more H2 styling cues. Holt Ware says a "bake off" was held between H1 and H2 designs with a decision made to focus on incorporating more of the H2 into the final H3 styling.

NOT VERY MANY DAYS AFTER THAT AUTO SHOW, CLAY DEAN RECRUITED HOLT WARE to join his new HUMMER studio. Dean asked Ware to begin work on the exterior of an all-new and still very secret future HUMMER model, the H3.

With the overwhelmingly positive reception enjoyed by the HUMMER H2 Vision concept, it might appear that designing the H3 meant simply applying the same styling cues to a smaller vehicle. But that would be far from what happened. Instead, between Ware's initial sketches and the final sign-off, the H3 design team would traverse territory as challenging as the Rubicon's Big Sluice Box and endure detours as daunting as Moab's Poison Spider Trail.

Ware and his colleagues explored a wide range of potential H3 designs: a low-priced, entry-level, two-door SUV with a hose-out interior and removable fenders; one with rear-hinged rear access doors and a reconfigurable truck bed/cargo area; a four-door SUV that retained nearly all the elements of the new Colorado/Canyon pickup platform; and an all-new SUV with the pickup truck's powertrain but with a HUMMER's upright windshield, wheels pushed as far as possible toward the corners, huge tires, and off-road capabilities unequalled in its segment, yet also with an interior befitting a vehicle that would be part of a premium brand.

"We wrung the process out to its fullest," says Jon Albert, a GM design veteran who was the H3 design

Even before the "Voice of Design" document was finished, the design for the GMT345 project focused on an entry-level utility vehicle with rear access doors and a rear section that could be reconfigured in several ways.

director and who focused on the H3 interior while Ware worked on the exterior. "We studied every permutation of HUMMER architecture we could."

Throughout calendar year 2000, the design team tackled overall vehicle architecture, explored a variety of reconfigurable HMMWV-style cargo-carrying possibilities, and considered how many and what kind of doors the H3 should have.

The first hurdle was trying to design a HUMMER around the architecture of the new Chevrolet Colorado/GMC Canyon midsize pickup truck. The Colorado/Canyon's GMT355 chassis might be terrific for a midsize pickup platform and provide everything anyone would expect of such a vehicle, but HUMMERs and HMMWVs look the way they do for a reason. To make their way over obstacles on the battlefield or the roughest of off-road trails, HUMMERs need ground clearance and big tires on wheels set at the far corners of the chassis.

Designers love big tires, especially when they fill the wheel wells and are pushed toward a vehicle's far corners, enhancing any vehicle's stance. Even the engineers agreed that to meet the demands of the off-road capability index

that GM established for the HUMMER brand, the H3 needed tires 33 inches tall—2 inches taller than the Colorado architecture was designed to accept. While they were at it, the axles that carried those wheels would have

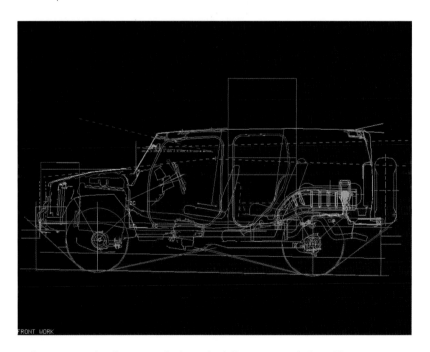

FRONT WORK

Holt Ware says chassis structure had a major influence on H3 design. This computer screen capture shows the vehicle packaging that had to be accommodated by the H3 design team.

to be well separated to reduce front and rear overhangs, which are anathemas for off-roading. Such changes would be expensive, but they also were necessary. "It was a win for the whole team," says Albert. "You got a much more purposeful-looking side-view proportion and you got the capability to go bigger on the tires."

The vertical windshield on the military Humvee reduces reflections that might signal the vehicle's position. The windshield on the H2 was strikingly upright as well. Designers wanted a similar look for the H3, even though it would increase tooling costs.

"From the outset, the chassis content had to be a huge driver for the styling," Ware explains. "If we didn't have the size, the tire capability, the dash-to-axle formula, the ground clearance, the right wheelbase, and all the other stuff, it wouldn't come off looking as purposeful as it does."

To meet its off-road performance criteria, the H3 needed a wide stance. HUMMERs, at least H1 and H2, have flat sides that extend to the vehicle's full width to

cover wheels and tires without flared fenders. But that design wouldn't be possible on the H3, which would be built in the same assembly line as the Colorado/Canyon. The new Shreveport plant had been specifically designed for pickup trucks and SUVs with sheet metal no wider than 1,690 millimeters. The only solution would be flared fenders.

Those fenders were a subject of concern and revision for many, many months, at least until the day when HUMMER general manager Mike DiGiovanni brought Arnold Schwarzenegger by to see how the H3 was progressing. Schwarzenegger was one of the first outsiders to see the design, and DiGiovanni was anxious about how he would react. Schwarzenegger came around the corner and stopped: "Ah, Mike, I love what you did with the fenders!" he said. It was as if the whole design team heaved a sigh of relief.

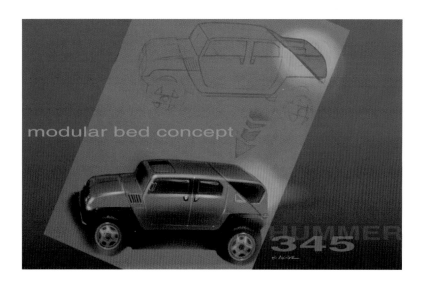

Designers considered myriad ideas for a reconfigurable cargo area.

A rough but full-size foam model was built to look at reconfigurable designs in full scale.

Each aspect of vehicle architecture caused its own anxieties. "When we started this there was more of an H1 philosophy," Ware says. Should the H3 look like a 9/10-scale version of the H2, or could it introduce new design features to the HUMMER brand? The design team was concerned about falling into a "Russian doll syndrome" in which the H3—and any subsequent HUMMERs—would simply be scaled-down versions of the H2, thus locking the brand into an inflexible format.

To avoid stylistic confinement, the design team experimented with themes closer to H1 than H2. The military version of the H1—the M998A2 High-Mobility Multipurpose Wheeled Vehicle (HMMWV) or Humvee— was available in a variety of configurations: a base platform with no doors, a two-door cargo/troop carrier with either an open or covered area, a four-door and slope-backed armament/tow missile carrier, a shelter carrier with an L-shaped shipping cube behind its two-door cab, and hard- or soft-top ambulance versions.

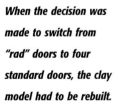

When the decision was made to switch from "rad" doors to four standard doors, the clay model had to be rebuilt.

The H3 design team explored an H1-like reconfigurable cargo area, with a structural buttress behind the passenger compartment and an open bed. The back end was designed to accept any of several modular options, including a removable SUV-style hard square back, a slope back, a canvas top, and a pass-through like the one that was under development for debut in the summer of 2001 on the Chevrolet Avalanche sport utility truck.

Adding impetus to this sport utility truck approach for the H3 was the fact that Clay Dean's original drawings for the H2 concept vehicle had a pickup bed in back, not an SUV-style roof over the cargo area. Dean changed his design to a full SUV after learning that

GM's agreement with AM General specified that this "son of HUMMER" would be a standard sport utility, not something with an open bed.

However, there were no such restrictions on the H3.

"We even built a buck; a seating buck that had all the flip and fold stuff," says Jon Albert. The buck was made of wood and went through several iterations—two doors, two doors with two rear access doors, four regular doors. The buck was used by designers, engineers, product planners, and even by focus group participants to evaluate ease of entry and exit, the relationship between various seating positions and the instrument panel, and structural roof pillar locations. It also served as a platform for experimenting with the myriad cargo-area configurations.

These illustrations show the evolution of the H1-oriented design theme that was considered for the H3.

These illustrations show the evolution of the H2-oriented design theme that was considered for the H3.

Focus groups found the cargo configurations overwhelming, even confusing. "The HUMMER appearance is so bold as it is, and then you start adding on top all this different functionality and reconfigurability— it was just overloading," says Ware.

"We loaded too many toppings on the enchilada," Albert agrees.

A single, well-designed cargo area with HUMMER styling cues, along with four standard doors, was the solution.

Unless they were so long as to alter vehicle proportions, two doors couldn't provide sufficient access to the back seat. The design team held out for RAD (rear access doors) as long as possible, at least until engineers explained that such architecture caused concerns about

diminished torsional rigidity. Imagine, Albert says, your SUV has carried you to the end of the trail, and now its rear access doors won't open.

While each aspect of design seemed to include its own set of detours, the exploration of interchangeable cargo configurations and various door options and all the rest was neither a waste of time nor of money. Sometimes the best way to learn what a model's core values are is to push well beyond them and let the vehicle's essence pull you back.

As Dean explains, "When they went as far as they did, it wasn't because they were trying to reinvent; it was because H3 was targeted to a younger audience and we didn't want to do the papa-mama-baby-bear strategy."

But the realization came that at this point in the development of the HUMMER brand, the H3 needed to build on the equity that was developing with the impending launch of H2.

"There are a lot of people who won't buy an H2 because it is either too big or it's too expensive or whatever," says Dean. "When we get four, five, and even six different vehicles out there, we're going to be able to have some that are very extreme. We'll be able to push the envelope further and further out and be more aggressive."

And many of the possibilities explored on H3 will provide fodder for the future. "We definitely learned with that," says Dean. "We'll be able to pull that experience with us as we continue to go forward and identify where to go next with other HUMMER vehicles."

THE H3 NEEDED TO GO MORE TOWARD H2 STYLING CUES, though again there would be many iterations of fenders, hoods, and grille designs, even adventures with air boxes, an iconic design cue located nea the base of the windshield pillars on the H1 and H2.

"We had a lot of work around the slots and lamps and the angle and attitude of the front centerline of the grille," Ware recalls. The design was pushed a little too far, and the concept began to lose its signature look; round headlights that compress the seven grille slots are a HUMMER design cue. So they took out a 5-gallon bucket of Bondo and started going to town on the full-scale clay model.

Dean says that the team created some wild images and fresh new ideas, but that they were not true to the developing HUMMER identity. "Because we were really a brand in infancy, it was wise to advance the form language and visual clues that the public was going to identify with the brand. We kind of backtracked a little bit and established forms and gestures that very much key off what is on the H2. But the H3 remains unique because we have these fenders that are standing outside the vehicle, and it also is more refined, surfacewise and detailwise. It's a little more finessed."

Working together over three months, Dean and Ware reworked such major details as the grille, windshield header, window shapes, and tail treatment. They even made the body sides more vertical ("pushed out the

For the "bake off" to decide which theme the H3 would take, clay models of the H2- and H1-based versions were prepared for a side-by-side showdown.

After the "bake off," Holt Ware focused on designing what would become the production version of the HUMMER H3.

tumblehome" in designer speak). By the time they were finished, the H3 had come a surprising full circle.

Dean gives a lot of credit to Ware. "Holt is awesome, just a great designer, smart, shrewd," says Dean. "What's intriguing is that some of Holt's original sketches, when he first started, are really where we ended up."

"We gave the architectural engineers a panic attack, and it was right on the border of DSO [Design Sign Off] and it was kind of crazy, but it was worth it," says Ware.

Design Sign Off is the point at which the design department signs off on styling; this occurs six to eight weeks before CSO [Contract Sign Off], at which point vice presidents put their signatures on paper. "Once you're past that point," says Albert, "concrete is being poured, tooling steel is being cut, contracts with suppliers are being signed, and workers are being hired."

"Can you imagine," adds Ware, "that at DSO we changed the air box and the whole hood hinge and unsprung the tumblehome even more, restruck the whole body side? We had six to eight weeks to pull all that together before CSO. There were some really tense moments there."

Finally, however, the H3 had the right form vocabulary and details, at least on the outside.

HUMMER

The final design of the HUMMER H3 takes shape as a design illustration and in clay.

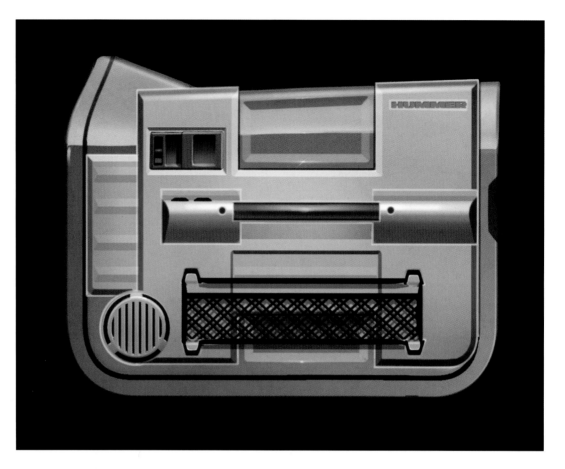

Early interior design studies emphasized metallic or painted surfaces.

IP SKETCH

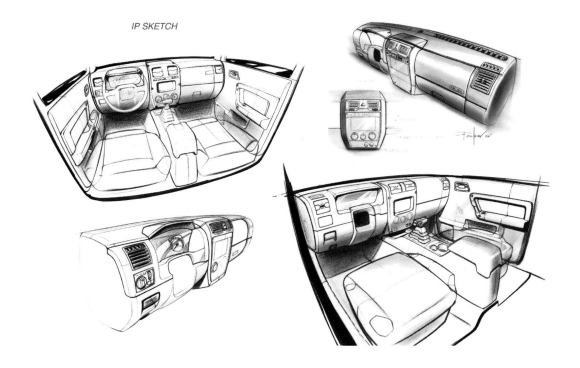

Interior design moved toward providing a more upscale environment. Design and engineering worked closely to devise air vents that provided a smooth, flush finish when closed.

AIRVENT

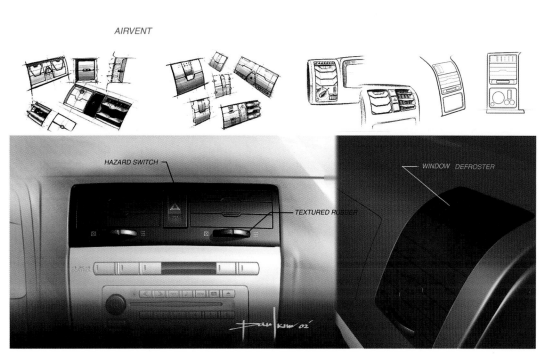

HAZARD SWITCH

TEXTURED RUBBER

WINDOW DEFROSTER

"YOU CAN MAKE IT LOOK LIKE A GARBAGE TRUCK ON THE OUTSIDE, but it has to look like a Bentley on the interior." That's what Bob Lutz told the H3 design team not long after he joined General Motors as vice chairman and product guru in September 2001.

Initial interior designs focused on low-cost options and looked at hose-out interiors, painted metal and steel interiors with exposed fasteners, aggressive angular seating, removable doors, and the like.

"We went to Mishawaka and got to see Humvees being built, and we loved the fact that there was this aesthetic—a military-engineered appearance—and we wanted to try to get that factored into the H3," says Albert. "We had aggressive corrugated shapes going on,

The HUMMER H3's interior provides a comfortable environment with pleasing tones and textures and switchgear that is intuitive in its placement and function.

stamped into the doors, molded into the consoles. But the people that we were going to ask to make payments couldn't relate to it. It became very clear that people wanted comfort and luxury on the inside and the rugged hardware approach on the outside.

"Ultimately," continues Albert, "we focused on just a very clean, straightforward surface vocabulary that had a lot of focus on premium quality of materials. It was basically a 180-degree reversal of what we tried to explore early on."

In the spring of 2002, Dave Lyon joined the HUMMER design team to help with the new interior. Lyon had been chief designer in Buick's brand character studio and was responsible for the gorgeous Buick Bengal roadster concept car in 2001.

"He had a great sense for elegance, but he also knew how to temper that so it had the right level of execution for this vehicle," says Albert of Lyon. "That was the right vein of what the mood of our vehicle needed to be on the inside."

The seats—available in cloth or leather—add to the visual appeal. With color-contrasted welting, seats are available with an interplay of ebony bolsters with cashmere- or morocco-colored cushion and back inserts.

A material called "Nissha" was selected for the center stack and instrument cluster frame. Commonly used in the electronics industry, Nissha looks like brushed aluminum and allows for high-quality finish execution, with easy changes for special-edition variants and model updates.

The interior floors are not rubber, but the rear load area is. The philosophy of the interior is to have a premium flavor all the way to the back of the back seat, and from there rearward to retain the sort of rugged utility the team pursued early in the program. Owners can get it dirty and it will hold up and clean up easily. The back of the rear seat is a hard panel that the owners can load things on and not worry.

"You can do luxury that is extremely functional," Dean notes. And that's exactly what the HUMMER H3 demanded—an authentic descendant of the military Humvee translated into a vehicle for civilians to use on an everyday basis.

"It's a great thing as a designer that you could make arguments to the engineering team and win those arguments because that's what HUMMER deserves, that's what is expected of a HUMMER. 'This is what we should be doing, why are you questioning it?'" says Dean. "We even used that argument with Bob Lutz and we'd win. It's pretty neat when the essence of your brand has that kind of power, to compel people internally to make significant investment in things that they might not do with a Chevrolet truck."

"Authentic HUMMER," says Albert. "A lot of the tradeoffs we made for the fundamental architecture and chassis design worked to our benefit in the final design statement."

The design process was far from over. There would be ongoing exchanges during the vehicle development process. But now it was up to the engineers to put the H3 design into motion.

The interior design team opted for a color palette that was simple yet emphatic: all ebony, ebony and cashmere, or ebony and Morocco, a rich terra cotta color. The interior also got what the designers call a "visual waterline" with ebony dashand door panels and contrasting cashmere or Morocco accents.

"This does a good job of lending a visual drama that we think is appropriate for HUMMER and gives it a nice upscale flavor," says Albert.

Chapter 4

The 10 Percent Solution

Engineering the H3 for Action

"We don't want to have people calling us saying, 'My HUMMER won't go through the Rubicon.' Yes, it will!"

—*Kevin Dinger,*
H3 vehicle performance manager

The H3 may be smaller than its big brothers, but there's no mistaking that it's a HUMMER.

Snap! Crackle! Pop!

That's not your breakfast cereal sounding off. Those are axles, prop shafts, suspension mounts, and other vehicle components being brutalized beyond the breaking point by General Motors development engineers. These guys and gals push things to and past their limits, and then get out with their jacks, their wrenches, and their spare parts, lie on their backs on sharp boulders, in bitter snowstorms, in pouring rain, in blistering desert sun, at night, whenever, wherever, so the people who buy a HUMMER H3 won't have to.

"Obviously, when you get into serious off-road situations, you're going to drive a lot more than normal torque into singular components," says Kevin Dinger, vehicle performance manager during the development of the HUMMER H3.

Early in the H3 development program, suspension and drivetrain components were pushed to and beyond their breaking points as engineers worked to make sure parts would be strong enough to certify the H3 as a true HUMMER. This second-generation mule was halted while its right-front half shaft was replaced.

CANYON/COLORADO FRAME

H3 FRAME

❶ BUMPERS MOUNTED DIRECTLY TO FRAME RAILS

❷ ADDITIONAL CROSSMEMBERS FOR INCREASED LATERAL STRUCTURE

❸ BODY MOUNTS RELOCATED FOR INCREASED RIGIDITY

❹ HEAVY DUTY JOUNCE BUMPERS

❺ MOVED SPRING HANGERS FOR INCREASED GROUND CLEARANCE IN OFF-ROADING

"On some of the early off-road trips, we broke a lot of stuff: axle shafts, transfer cases, front differentials. You name it and we broke it," adds Tom Wallace, vehicle line executive for GM's small and midsize trucks and sport utility vehicles.

"There were loads here we had never seen before," adds Dinger. "You get a wheel spinning and then suddenly it grabs and . . . " Snap! Crackle! Pop!

When General Motors' North American Strategy Board approved the design, development, and production of the HUMMER H3, it requested that 70 percent of the parts and pieces come directly from the company's new Chevrolet Colorado/GMC Canyon midsize pickup trucks. After all, that's how sport utility vehicles typically are developed—from a pickup truck foundation vehicle.

HUMMERs, however, are not your typical SUVs.

By the time Dinger and the engineering design and development team finished, only 10 percent of what makes up a Colorado/Canyon remains part of the H3, and the engine, transmission, seat structure, and toe pan (the sheetmetal panel that runs from beneath the front seats and pedals to just ahead of the instrument panel) comprise the vast majority of that commonality.

It's not that the Colorado and Canyon aren't good, solid vehicles. Like Dinger, many of the engineers who developed the H3 also worked on the pickups, known within GM as GMT355. Equipped with the optional Z71 off-road suspension package, Colorado and Canyon are more than capable on trails that off-road guidebooks warn "may be impassable for inexperienced drivers."

But the thing is, "impassable" isn't part of the HUMMER vocabulary.

"WE REALLY SET SOME AGGRESSIVE TARGETS FOR OFF-ROAD PERFORMANCE," says Dinger.

Though based on the underpinnings of the Colorado/Canyon pickup truck, the frame for the HUMMER H3 underwent substantial beefing up.

Complicating the pursuit of those targets was the need to achieve them without detracting from the on-road ride and handling, the control and comfort that people expect from a premium sport utility vehicle. That the H3 would be a first for the HUMMER brand—a mainstream GM development program, not a joint-venture, skunk-works, H2-style effort with the off-road specialists from AM General—only added to the challenge.

Sure, engineers who developed the H2 and experts from AM General could be counted on for help, but the H3 development team had to get itself up to speed off-road if its vehicle was going to live up to its HUMMER badge.

While GM did not have as strong a corporate heritage in extreme off-roading as some of its automaker rivals—GM didn't offer factory-installed four-wheel-drive until the late 1950s, and even afterward people who were serious about off-roading opted for Jeeps, Fords, and Range and Land Rovers—there were engineers at GM's Michigan and Arizona proving grounds who were expert off-roaders. They helped gather other experts and engineers from top off-road aftermarket suppliers for mud-slinging, rock-climbing educational field trips for the H3 development team.

On its early trials, the team took along vehicles that the H3 would have to exceed in off-road capability, as well as a specially modified Chevrolet Blazer with a 3-inch Superlift kit, ARB front and rear air-locker differentials, and off-road wheels and tires.

Package illustrations show the positions of major mechanical components such as engine, transmission, suspension and the clearances needed for them to fit properly. The positions of driver and other occupants are included in some views.

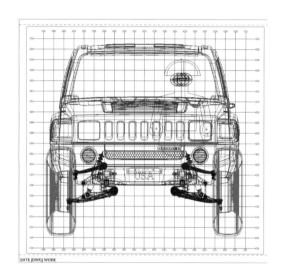

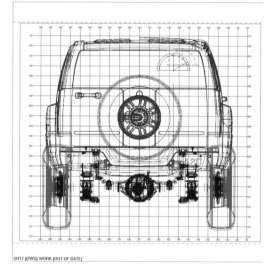

This schematic shows the details of the H3 passenger compartment and allows engineers to examine such things as pedal travel, steering wheel angle, and many other features in a virtual model.

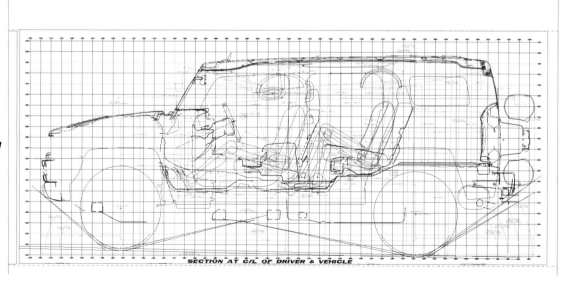

SECTION AT C/L OF DRIVER & VEHICLE

The team also went through the extreme off-road driving program conducted on "the infield" at HUMMER headquarters in northern Indiana, where the man-made obstacles were designed to challenge even the HMMWV.

The team returned home to the GM tech center in Warren, Michigan, with a mission: To build an H3 that would exceed not only factory-built competitors but many highly customized off-road vehicles such as the team's own modified Blazer.

. "We don't want to have people calling us saying, 'My HUMMER won't go through the Rubicon,'" Dinger says. "Yes, it will!" he adds with confidence born of several trips down that and other trails.

BUT GETTING FROM COLORADO TO THE END OF THE RUBICON TRAIL was a challenging task.

"Design and engineering go on simultaneously," explains Brooks Stover, vehicle line director for H3.

Stover had day-to-day responsibility for H3 engineering and development.

"There's a sequence where design has a chance to express what they would like to do," Stover continues. "In fact, they create a document called 'The Voice of Design.' It's their free expression of what they would like to see in this vehicle—the things they'd fall on their swords for, like big tires at the corners, vertical windshield, slab sides, interior, and so on."

In parallel with the design development goals, engineering sets its own parameters. "We have to be best off-road," says Stover, "so I have a certain ground clearance, the appropriate tire sizes . . . "

The engine that would power the H3 was established early. The base engine for start of production would be the five-cylinder 3500 Vortec.

"Like every program," Stover says, "you like to have an up-level powertrain, and we have some in the plan. We know we don't have an exorbitant amount of power,

A HUMMER prototype shows its strength and its maneuverability in tight quarters during a drive down the Rubicon Trail in September 2003.

but we do have a 4.56 rear axle that gives you a nice launch feel, and when you drive the truck, this powertrain is perfectly consistent with the HUMMER brand character."

The H3 isn't about 0–60 mile-per-hour sprint times; it's about climbing from flat surfaces to 60 percent grades.

The Vortec 3500 provides 220 horsepower and 225 ft-lbs of torque. The engineering team especially liked it

for two reasons that have nothing to do with its power: It is neither too heavy nor too long.

"People have said, 'Why didn't you put the inline six in it?'" Stover says, referring to the 275-horsepower Vortec 4200 used in the Chevrolet TrailBlazer and other larger SUVs. The answer comes down to weight and length. Extending the HUMMER's nose to accommodate the longer engine would affect off-road capabilities.

This rolling chassis shows the strength of the frame, the sturdiness of the suspension components, and the layout of the powertrain that lies beneath the H3. **Larry Edsall**

"We wanted the approach angle that we have, which is high 30s," says Stover. "To add another cylinder, the nose gets longer. Any shortcoming [in raw horsepower] is more than offset by how agile the truck is. Popping around corners, turning the corner and getting going, you hit the throttle and you're off. You get the feeling you're driving a very sporty vehicle."

"Having it smaller, lighter, more maneuverable—the versatility that it gives off-road is wonderful," says Lori Cumming, vehicle chief engineer for GM's small and midsize trucks and SUVs, including the H3. "It's just nimble and fun to drive off-road."

And, notes Stover, the H3 gets up to 20 miles per gallon on the highway.

JUST AS THE H3 DESIGN STAFF HAD TO MAKE A BOLD STYLING STATEMENT in keeping with the iconic cues established by the HMMWV, the HUMMER H1, and the HUMMER H2, the engineering team's guiding principle was off-road capability.

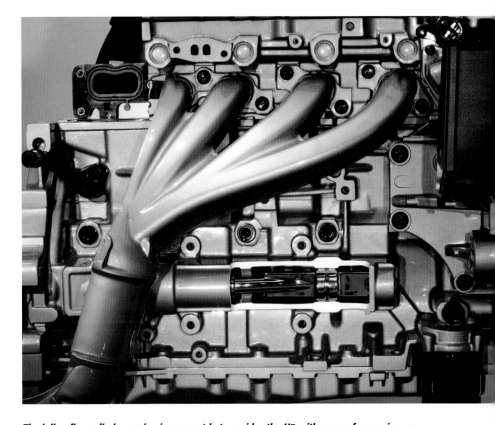

The inline five-cylinder engine is compact but provides the H3 with power for passing on the highway and for muscling its way over rough, unpaved terrain.

"Everyone lined up behind the requirements," adds Cumming. "It's harder to make decisions when the vision of what the product needs to be is not as clear. With the HUMMER, the right answer just is obvious."

Obvious, perhaps, but not necessarily easy to execute, nor inexpensive. Design and development of the H3 would cost GM almost twice as much as a standard pickup-to-SUV, Blazer-style vehicle.

The braking system provides one of many examples: The Colorado/Canyon has front disc and rear drum brakes and uses a conventional vacuum-boost master brake cylinder that draws power from vacuum created by the engine. Such a system works fine in normal applications. But the H3 is not a normal application. Its gross vehicle weight rating is 500 pounds more than the pickup truck's. It also has much larger tires. Therefore, its braking system must deal with considerably greater forces in vehicle dynamics and rotating masses.

To meet its targets for off- and on-pavement performance, the H3 team needed an upgrade. It opted for an electro-hydraulic system grabbing four-wheel discs—each more than a foot in diameter—with four-piston front calipers and a sliding single piston in the rear. The system incorporates anti-lock technology, traction control, and electronic stability control as well.

This braking system is completely new for General Motors. So is the supplier, ADVICS North America, which is owned by a consortium of Japanese auto suppliers Denso, Aisin Seiko, and Sumitomo Electric, and which made its name as a primary supplier to Toyota.

"It's pretty expensive hardware," says H3 chief brake engineer Rob Fritsch, "but it's terrific technology. The four-piston calipers and electro-hydraulics are the key. This electro-hydraulic unit is a self-contained electric pump. It builds pressure in an accumulator and through electrical power provides its own assist." While the standard system is limited by engine vacuum, the electro-hydraulic unit is limited only by on-board computing power.

"We get maybe a thirty to forty percent higher boost capacity," Fritsch explains, "and because the chassis control module is integral to the unit, it has really good response times for vehicle stability. It has brake intervention, traction control, and it's capable of responding very quickly."

"You don't realize how important that is until you're on a trail and you have three wheels spinning and only one with traction," explains Jenna Pechauer, vehicle dynamics controls performance engineer for the H3. The technology will quickly apply the brake to the spinning wheels and transfer any torque to the one wheel that

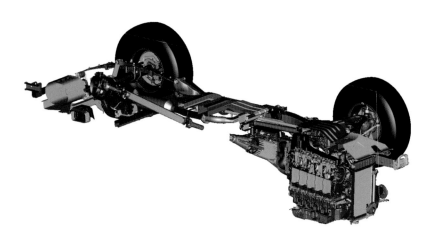

Using the computer allows engineers to examine the H3 frame and drivetrain components from various angles, even upside down. This is important since the frame is upside down during much of the vehicle's initial assembly process.

1. MASTER AND BOOST BRAKE APPLY SYSTEM
2. CHASSIS CONTROL MODULE (**EHCU**)
3. INERTIAL SENSOR (YAW AND LATERAL)
4. WHEEL SPEED SENSORS (4)
5. INSTRUMENT CLUSTER
6. POWERTRAIN CONTROL MODULE
7. THROTTLE PEDAL POSITION SENSOR
8. BODY CONTROL MODULE
9. STEERING WHEEL SENSOR
10. TRACTION CONTROL ON/OFF SWITCH
— HYDRAULIC CIRCUITS
— ELECTRICAL CIRCUITS

The HUMMER H3 is the first GM vehicle to feature an integrated stability, braking, and traction control system by automotive supplier ADVICS North America.

has traction. The longer it takes to do that, the more momentum the tires and wheels build up and the harder it is to regain any kind of control.

"On this vehicle we have a rear-locking differential but at this point we do not have a front locker, so that makes the brake traction even more critical," Pechauer continues. "Truly, that's the only way we can get single-wheel traction."

While ADVICS had done electro-hydraulic systems for the Toyota 4Runner, it hadn't been asked to meet the sort of challenges an H3 is expected to face. The H3 team took the engineers from the brake and traction system supplier along on one of its trips to Moab, Utah, where it introduced ADVICS to the Golden Crack.

"It's a giant crevasse, and you have to take just the right line through it," Pechauer says. Even then, "you have two wheels in the air almost at all times."

The first crack at the Golden Crack didn't go very well. The traction system didn't perform as expected and the truck wasn't able to move forward. Months later, after the system had been retuned, everyone went back to the Crack.

"I told the guys I was driving through this obstacle first because I wanted to see how the revised system did," Pechauer says. "They took me through the most brutal line you can take and that truck was literally rocking back and forth and side to side, but the traction system kicked in perfectly. The wheels didn't spin up. As soon as they started to spin, the system grabbed on, transferring the torque, and we crawled right through. It's a very capable off-road vehicle."

In addition to working so well in extreme off-pavement conditions, the system includes vehicle stability control for better on-pavement balance. This enhances the H3's performance in the National Highway Traffic Safety Administration's "fish-hook" test, used to judge an SUV's tendency to roll over in emergency maneuvers.

"For our vehicle, we'll have three 175-pound water dummies in the back seat, a driver dummy, and a steering robot and equipment, which weighs 50 to 75 pounds more, in the passenger seat," Pechauer says. "This maneuver is brutal. You have to use a steering robot because a human can't physically do it as smoothly and as well."

The steering dummy acts like the ultimate Hollywood stunt driver. The vehicle accelerates to 50 miles per hour

Computers allow engineers to peel away the sheet metal for an x-ray view of the H3 chassis.

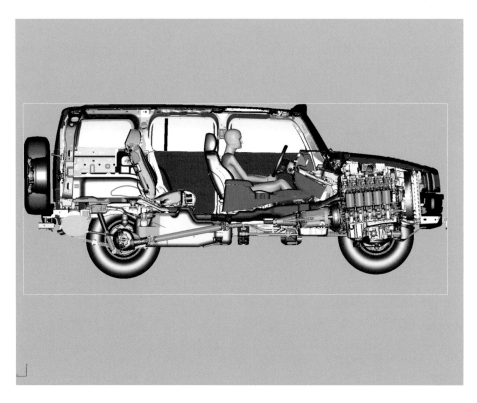

The D rings on the HUMMER H2 are basically U bolts with a constant section, but designers wanted something more for the H3, so they worked with engineering, creating math models and prototypes to make sure they'd be both aesthetically pleasing and strong enough to carry significant loads—each ring can support the vehicle's full weight. "We worked back and forth probably on eight iterations between design and structural engineering," says Brooks Stover. The result: The rings look good, are strong, and become standard equipment not only on the H3 but on the H2 as well. **Brenda Priddy & Company**

and the dummy turns the wheel in one direction. Just as the vehicle reaches its peak point of lean, the robot cranks the wheel in the opposite direction to induce a rollover, or at least a tip-up, wheels-in-the-air situation.

"The faster response times of this [braking and stability] system really help in being able to control the vehicle before it gets out of control," Pechauer says.

A lesser system might be able to respond properly, she adds, but to do so it would have to be engineered to be more intrusive, even in an ordinary lane-change maneuver; the software would have to engage earlier just in case the lane change intensifies into something more severe.

One way to do that is to severely reduce engine torque. However, this can create a situation in which a driver makes a maneuver to avoid an accident, only to find the vehicle in jeopardy of being struck while the driver waits for the engine to spin back up into its power band.

"When the driver turns the steering wheel, we want the system to be able to help the vehicle go where the driver's telling it to go," Pechauer says. "It's a safety system, first and foremost. But beyond that, you don't want to take anything away from the driving experience. That's the balance that we're constantly looking at."

ALL OF THE EARLY-IN-THE-PROGRAM DECISIONS RESULTED IN what the engineers call the "criteria." What comes next is a detailed, painstaking analysis and integration of design's voice and engineering's criteria.

As this engineering screen capture shows, the D rings connect directly to the front of the H3 frame.

Computers provide engineers with many ways to look inside their work. This is a worm's-eye view of the inner workings of the H3. Components can be colored by system, material, or for their aerodynamic or thermal qualities.

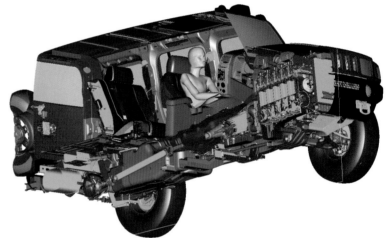

Computer-aided engineering helps make sure that all H3 underbody components are protected by sturdy shielding or tucked up and out of harm's way.

In a vehicle such as the H3, "there are maybe 400 of what we call 'typical sections,'" Brooks Stover explains. Engineering analyzes each section to determine what characteristics it must have to allow the whole vehicle to perform as required. For example, engineering might determine that a particular section of rocker panel has to display a particular rigidity, or resistance to bending. Engineering takes that requirement to manufacturing, which has a better vision of the particular assembly methods the factory will use. Together they learn how to apply available methods and materials to achieve the required performance.

That's just the beginning. Then the iterative process begins. Design Center takes the section and puts it on its clay model. The part that satisfies engineering's strength requirements and manufacturing's method of construction may create visual changes that the design department doesn't like. Design then indicates what it wants to see, engineering explains the limitations it and manufacturing have identified, and they negotiate. This trading off occurs for each of those hundreds of sections.

Stover, who has degrees in engineering and design, understands both perspectives. "We get agreement on the sections at the bottom of the vehicle first and work to the top," Stover explains. They build from the bottom for two reasons: first, to clear major hurdles like barrier crash tests that determine whether or not the program can go forward. Second, lower-chassis parts require the longest time for pre-production tooling. Once those sections are squared away, their development process can commence while the team moves on to other sections. Eventually the players reach agreement on all of the hundreds of sections of the vehicle.

"Shortly after that," says Stover, "we freeze the clay and the surface is set." But even then details can change right up to the start of production. There can even be running changes on the assembly line.

But long before the first H3 starts its way along the line at Shreveport, prototype vehicles need to be built and tested. Parts that aren't stout enough must be redesigned, then fabricated, tested, and retested again

Bridgestone uses three plies of material in both the tread and sidewalls on the special off-road tire it designed for the H3.

and again. Tires must be developed. Someone has to figure out a way to mount the spare tire on the back of the vehicle. Someone else has to engineer a way to get the hood, grille, and cowl at the base of the windshield to progress from complex design sketches to production-line feasibility. Fenders are an on-going issue, and not just the fenders themselves but even the color of the gasket that fits between the fenders and the H3's sheetmetal bodywork.

THE H3 TEAM STARTS ITS DEVELOPMENT WORK WITH WHAT THE auto industry calls "mules"-very basic vehicles used to begin evaluation of various components. In the case of the HUMMER H3, these first-generation mules are red, two-door GMT355 pickup trucks with plastic front fender blisters and plastic "toppers" over their cargo beds. Built in the Pre-Production Operations (PPO) facility at GM's Validation Center in Pontiac, Michigan, the first mules were available to the team in the fall of 2001.

Second-generation mules—also built at PPO and available beginning in the summer of 2002—are black four-door sport utility vehicles designed to verify structural architecture and for continued component testing.

Next come 78 "integration" prototypes, vehicles also built at Pontiac, but now H3-specific with what is known as "production intent" structure and components. The first integration prototype was ready in November 2003. Half of the vehicles will be used for barrier-impact and

To begin evaluation of components that might be used in the HUMMER H3, the Product Execution Team (known within GM as the PET team) takes modified Colorado and Canyon pickup trucks to facilities maintained by AM General in northern Indiana to see whether such mules can climb a 60-percent grade and negotiate an obstacle known as the "mudslide."

Second-generation H3 mules are available in the summer of 2002, about the time designers are working to finish clay models of the future H3. These new mules are built as four-door sport utility vehicles for structural evaluation and component analysis. Their first challenge: the Rubicon Trail.

Tom Wallace, vehicle line executive in charge of HUMMER H3 design and development, participates in an engineering drive on the Rubicon Trail in August 2004.

occupant-protection crash testing, the others for on- and off-road product development and validation.

Finally, 30 "non-saleable units" were built on the assembly line at Shreveport to verify the assembly line production process. These vehicles went through final verification tests and were displayed at auto shows, beginning with the California International Auto Show at Anaheim, where the H3 was officially unveiled to the public at that show on October 27, 2004. These vehicles are also used for events such as media test drives.

"THERE ARE TWO THINGS ABOUT THIS TRUCK THAT REALLY HAVE BEEN CHALLENGES," says Brooks Stover. Both of them involve the H3's hood.

The HUMMER H1 and H2's hoods are hinged in front and open clamshell-style rather than like an alligator's mouth. But because of architecture and the assembly facilities that the H3 shares with the Colorado/Canyon pickup trucks, the H3's hood would have to be hinged near the base of the windshield. It also would be made from stamped steel rather than a lighter-weight and moldable composite material.

HUMMER H3 "integration prototypes" meet the challenges provided by the Rubicon Trail in August 2004.

To maintain iconic design similarity with its big brothers, the H3's hood had to incorporate a set of louvers in its surface and had to be shaped to accommodate air boxes near the base of the windshield support pillars, right where the hood hinges would normally be placed. It also had to fit with exact precision, flush with and positioned between an upright grille and a body-colored panel along the base of the windshield.

On a typical SUV or other passenger vehicle, the front edge of the hood wraps over the vehicle's nose and sits above the top of the grille and radiator while the rear edge of the hood sits above a plastic panel that includes the bases for the windshield wipers.

"Look at this truck," Stover says, pointing to a photograph of a Chevrolet TrailBlazer. "This hood can float between this edge and the overhangs here, so if it's off a millimeter or two, fore or aft, it's not going to be very obvious. But we have a trapped hood; it's trapped between the cowl screen and the grille, so the build tolerances are critical because there's no adjustment once the grille is in place and that cowl screen is in place."

As if that wasn't enough of a challenge, "We have another issue that's complicated it," says Stover. To provide both a strong appearance and structure, the front edge of the hood has what is known as a "hem flange," and unless the hood fits precisely, it can look as though the hood is ajar even when it is closed. "So now not only do we have to make it accurate in the fore/aft dimension, we have to make it uniform in up/down position.

"From a manufacturing standpoint," Stover explains, "styling managed to create about as complicated a front end as could be created. We look just like an H2, but the H2 is one big fiberglass piece so they don't have the issue of the hood stacking up to the cowl or the hood stacking up to the grille. They just mold that all in one chunk, and it tips forward."

The trapped hood design presented another problem. The typical vehicle hood is fairly flat and is designed to fold like an accordion in a frontal collision. But the H3 hood has a significant crown. It did not crumple in the front-end barrier crash test. Instead, enough force was transmitted rearward to break the hood hinges.

Accompanied by a HUMMER H2 as a support vehicle, a convoy of second-generation H3 mules makes its way along a trail near Moab, Utah.

Crawl ratios are vital not only for climbing hills but also for descending them safely.

Moab's Golden Crack is a daunting challenge even for this H3 mule during an engineering development trip in May 2003.

A stop at the top of the hill helps a driver find the best route up a Moab hill.

To meet designers' desires and engineers' criteria, the H3 needed to carry its spare tire on its rear door. Providing strong hinges and the structure to support them was a challenge met by engineering, which then made opening and closing the tire-weighted door easier by adding a gas strut. Brenda Priddy & Company; Larry Edsall

"A design that had been released [for production] had to be re-engineered," says Stover. "At the eleventh hour the guys had to do some significant work on the hinges."

THE H3 HOOD MAY HAVE BEEN A MAJOR ISSUE, BUT IT WASN'T THE ONLY ONE. For example, designers wanted the spare tire somewhere other than inside the H3's cargo area, and the typical under-vehicle location used on pickup trucks and many SUVs would inhibit the departure angle needed for serious off-roading. The solution was to mount the extra wheel and tire on the H3's rear door.

"It was a major push to get the tire on the back of the swing gate," says H3 designer Holt Ware. Again,

achieving the solution would be complicated by several factors, including the weight of the H3's large off-road wheel and tire, the rear gate still had to be easy to open and close, the hinges had to be strong enough to handle

Cutaway illustrations show front and rear suspension components in detail.

the gate and such weight, and everything still had to be aesthetically pleasing.

"The engineering team went through an incredible, monumental job," says H3 chief designer Jon Albert. "When you open that swing gate now, those hinges look like they could hold a 16-foot farm fence."

"WE GOT EVERYTHING WE WANTED IN ENGINEERING, and I've told the design guys they got everything they wanted, too. Everything!" says Brooks Stover.

The H3 is available with either a four-speed automatic or a five-speed manual transmission that extreme off-roaders will prefer. The Borg-Warner two-speed, electronically controlled, full-time four-wheel-drive system has a standard 2.64:1 low-range gear reduction,

and a 4.03:1 gear is available. A rear locking differential is available with either the 2.64:1 or the 4.03:1 transfer case.

Manual or automatic gearboxes can be set to "4High Open" for highway driving, "4High Locked" for a fixed torque split between the front and rear axles, or "4Low Locked" for severe off-pavement use. Packaged with the optional 4:1 transfer case is a locking rear differential for maximum traction in the most severe conditions and a crawl ratio as high as 69:1, which is higher than either the H1 or H2.

The H3 can climb 16-inch steps and ford water 2 feet deep. Just like the H1 and H2, it can handle a 60 percent grade and a 40 percent transverse.

"I remember the first time we were in Moab," says Tom Wallace, the H3 vehicle line executive who was a skilled sports car racer but who had very little off-road

This quintet of H3 integration mules made the trip down the Rubicon Trail in August 2004.

experience. "I said 'We're going up there?' The team said, 'Yep,' and there we went."

"You get people who maybe joined the team partway through the program or had just never been off-roading," adds Kevin Dinger. "They've seen the videos but they think it's trick photography. 'No way, you didn't really do that.' But you get them out there and they're just shocked, just blown away. The reaction is usually, 'Had I gotten to that point in the trail on my own, I would have turned around and gone home.'"

Several weeks before the start of production, "We took five of these down the Rubicon over a two-day period," says Wallace. "We had none, nada, zero failures. Nothing! Not even a flat tire."

The HUMMER H3 had been designed and engineered. Now it was up to Shreveport to get it built.

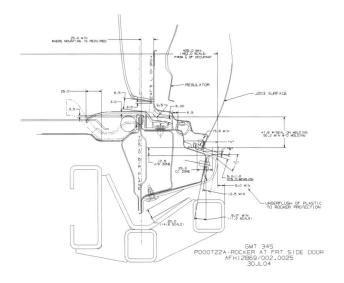

This cross-section of a portion of the H3 rocker panel is one of the hundreds of typical sections that designers and engineers must agree to as they create the new HUMMER. The reverse "C" shape at the lower left is part of the vehicle's frame. The red squares to the frame's right are optional rocker protection.

Chapter 5

Born on the Bayou

UAW 2166 Meets GMT345

"A HUMMER is not just a truck."

—Betsy Burke, second-shift supervisor of Shreveport's chassis line

Parts arrive in bins and are positioned in the proper sequence to coordinate with the vehicles as they travel down the assembly line. Neil Johnson

"The drop" takes place at 4:30 p.m. The "skillet" and its cargo are in motion.

This skillet isn't a frying pan, but a metal platform that carries a truck body shell as it travels along an X-shaped path through the four arms of the general assembly center that is part of the General Motors Truck Group's assembly plant in Shreveport, Louisiana.

The plant opened in 1981 to assemble GM's new compact pickup trucks, the Chevrolet S-10 pickup truck and its twin, the GMC Sonoma. Chevy Blazers and GMC Jimmys were also built at Shreveport. So was the GMC Syclone, the pickup truck that dusted Ferrari's 348ts, a genuine exotic sports car, a few years ago in a head-to-head test conducted by *Car and Driver* magazine.

With some 3,000 members of United Auto Workers (UAW) Local 2166 and some 200 salaried staff, the GM truck facility is the largest private employer in the Shreveport-Bossier area of northwestern Louisiana.

Shreveport is in Caddo Parish, which borders Texas to the west and Arkansas to the north. The Red River

The skeleton of the body shell for a HUMMER H3 begins to form in the Shreveport body plant. Neil Johnson

separates Caddo and Bossier Parishes. In northwestern Louisiana, only Barksdale Air Force Base in Bossier City has more "employees" than the GM plant, though healthcare, including the Louisiana State University medical school and several bio-med research facilities, enhances the quality of life in the bayou country along the riverbanks. The area also is home to the American Rose Center, the Independence Bowl football game, Louisiana Downs horse racing track, and three riverboat casinos.

Shreveport is named for Henry Miller Shreve, a steamboat captain who opened the area to development by leading the effort to clear the "Great Raft," a 165-mile logjam that clogged the Red River in the 1830s. Oil made Shreveport a boomtown in the 1900s.

In 1954, a young feller from Tupelo, Mississippi, moved to Shreveport. He had cut a couple of records up in Memphis, but he made his on-stage debut and immediately became a regular performer at Shreveport's Louisiana Hayride, a venue that was as important to what was known as "rockabilly" as Nashville's Grand Ole' Opry was to country and western.

Elvis Presley may have left the building, but Shreveport has discovered a new hometown hero, the HUMMER H3.

WHILE THE HUMMER H3 MAY SHARE ONLY 10 PERCENT OF ITS COMPONENTS with the Chevy Colorado

Doors produced in the nearby stamping plant are lined up, awaiting their turn to be attached to the shell of a HUMMER H3 in the Shreveport body shop. **Neil Johnson**

and GMC Canyon pickup trucks, it is built in the same plant, making Shreveport the only place outside of South Bend/Mishawaka, Indiana, to ever have produced a HUMMER (although GM eventually will use its Struandale assembly plant in South Africa to build as many as 10,000 H3s a year for overseas markets). Shreveport has produced a lot of trucks, but building the HUMMER has plant personnel excited.

"A HUMMER is not just a truck," says Betsy Burke, second-shift supervisor of Shreveport's chassis line.

"An icon" is what Jim Graham calls the H3. Graham was among the Shreveport UAW members sent to Michigan to work with GM engineers on H3 development and the vehicle's assembly process. Shreveport is especially excited, he says, because it gets to build the first HUMMER that is accessible to the sweet spot in the sport utility market, to middle-class consumers.

"There's a huge level of enthusiasm about this vehicle," says David Gibbons, the Shreveport plant

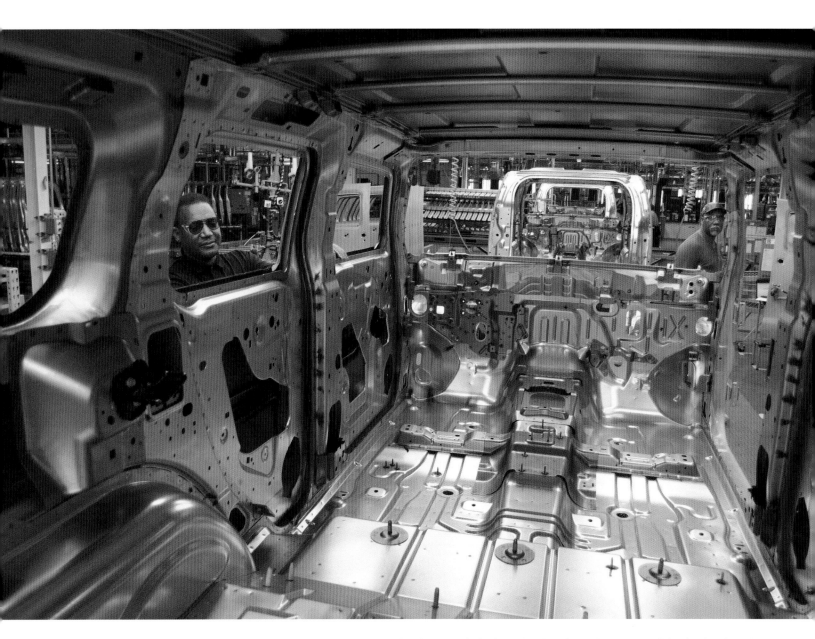

Left-side doors are attached as this H3 shell continues its way through the Shreveport body shop. This view shows the precision of the details achieved in the stamping process. **Neil Johnson**

manager. Gibbons explains that Shreveport is a state-of-the-art plant and a showcase for General Motors and its newest assembly processes, many of which were developed in Europe and brought to North America by some 400 Shreveport employees sent to Germany to study manufacturing techniques pioneered at Opel.

In the 1990s, GM invested more than $1 billion to build the new X-shaped general assembly facility and then spent another $250,000 to convert the older Shreveport plant into stamping and body assembly facilities for the H3.

The new Shreveport plant is laid out in a large "X" shape, with a series of truck bays along the outer rim of each axis so parts can be delivered adjacent to the place on the line where they will be installed. Installation is done at stations manned by a UAW team usually comprised of six members. Teams have authority to stop the line rather than to pass along any problems. Group and shift leaders are more enablers than supervisors in this production process.

Parts are delivered on a just-in-time basis from suppliers and other GM facilities. The exact sequence of vehicles along the assembly line—a mix of two brands of pickups, each with various cab configurations, as well as the H3 in each of its trim levels—is not determined until those vehicles leave the paint shop.

A sheetmetal shell gets close scrutiny as its moves through the body shop on its way toward the paint booth. Neil Johnson

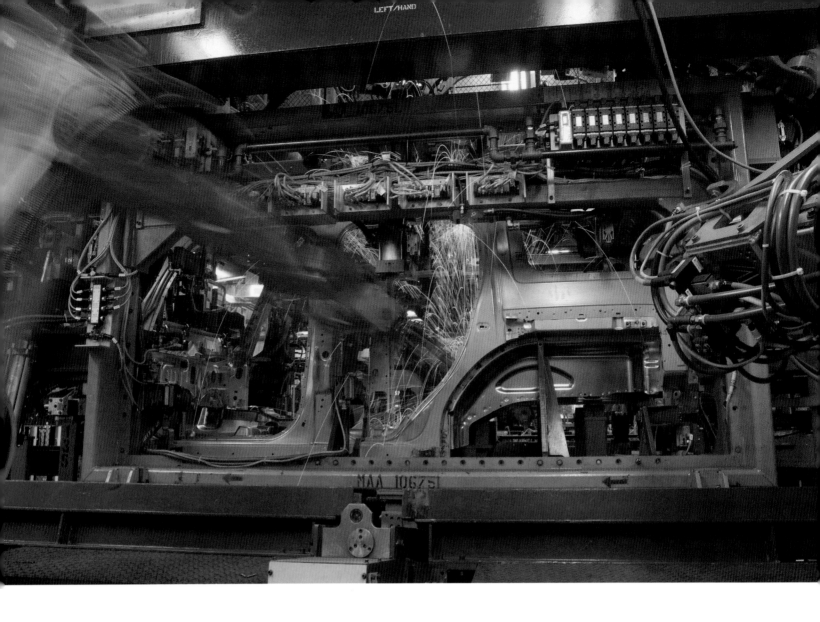

Robotic welders add panels to the exoskeleton of what is becoming a solid steel body of a HUMMER H3. Neil Johnson

The Shreveport facility covers 3.1 million square feet of floor space and has 28.7 miles of conveyors. It takes about an hour and a half for a vehicle to travel from the paint shop to the center of the general assembly center's X, where the body shell and its skillet drop onto the line. This means that suppliers have no more than 90 minutes—sometimes less—to deliver the right parts from their local facilities to the factory and to have them in the right sequence, lest a Colorado wind up with an H3 dashboard or an H3 with a Canyon's wheels and tires.

When the line is moving at full speed, it produces a vehicle every 72 seconds, or nearly 220,000 a year on two shifts. That gives the team at each workstation about 50 seconds to do its work before the skillet moves to the next station.

Watching the teams at work is like watching a finely choreographed NASCAR pit stop. Except that at Shreveport, the crew doesn't merely change wheels and

tires and refill the fuel tank, it builds up an entire vehicle from scratch. And then another. And another. And . . .

BECAUSE WE VISITED SHREVEPORT WHEN SALEABLE PRODUCTION UNITS of the H3 were first being built, the line wasn't moving at all-out racing speeds, at least not through every station. While the occasional slowdown may have provided educational if sometimes frustrating opportunities for the UAW workers, their group and shift leaders, and for the visiting engineers from Michigan, they provided a better view for outside observers. Thus, photographer Neil Johnson could stick his camera into places and I could ask questions of faces that would not be accessible when the line is at its full paces.

However, just like everyone else in the building, we were required to wear special belt buckle and wristwatch covers, lest we accidentally scratch a vehicle's paint.

On the day of our visit, H3s were being built on the second shift. An H3 "scout" vehicle made its drop onto the line behind several Colorados and Canyons at 4:30 p.m. When production is running at its regular pace, the sequence will be something like two trucks, an H3, two trucks, an H3, etc. But since H3 production was just getting started, the H3 scout would be followed by 30 pickups to provide time for evaluation and to make any changes needed before 14 more HUMMERs took their regular places in the rotation for the rest of the night's shift.

As expected, there were some hiccups. Items such as the H3's sunroof, headliner, and grille drew special attention. Several times, a UAW assembly team was outnumbered by engineers as the scout made its way along the line. But, says Doug Kast, a GM engineer and project manager for H3 production, "Having manufacturing working with our engineers and designers (for all those months in Michigan) pays big dividends" when it comes time to build the vehicle.

"This is our newest facility with all the latest and greatest (in vehicle assembly equipment)," Kast adds. "This plant has a history for its can-do attitude. Everyone is very responsive."

PRECISELY AT 4:30 P.M. CENTRAL TIME, A LARGE AND INDUSTRIAL-STRENGTH elevator rises inside its two-story

Roofs are welded into place. **Neil Johnson**

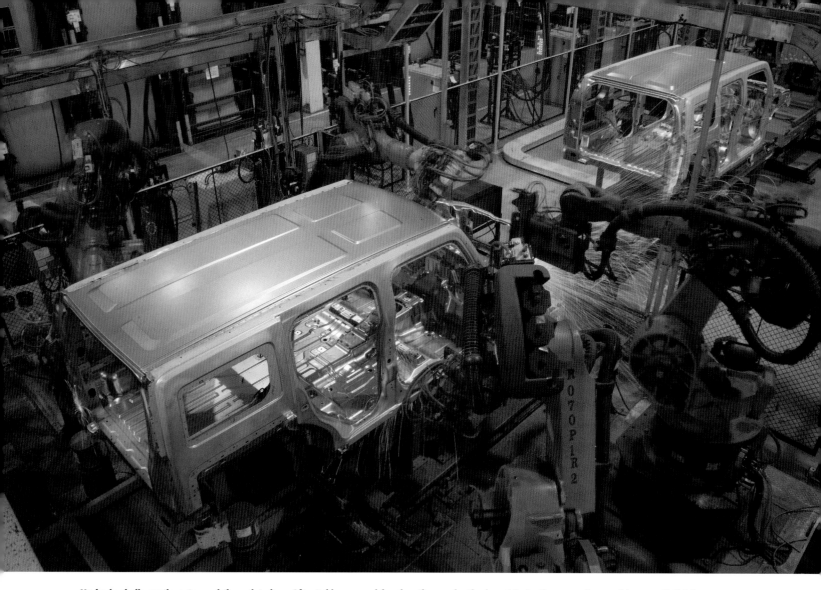

H3 body shells continue toward the paint shop. After taking on a rich color, they make the long trip to the general assembly area. Neil Johnson

Careful attention is paid to details such as fit and finish as the HUMMER H3 makes its way through the assembly process in Shreveport. Neil Johnson

Glass is heavy. To smooth installation of the sunroof, a mechanical arm helps maneuver the panel into place. Neil Johnson

To make installation of interior components easier, doors are removed from body shells in the general assembly plant. Neil Johnson

The doors go onto carriers that disappear into the rafters and then magically reappear later to be rejoined with their original vehicle. Neil Johnson

HVAC equipment—heat, ventilation, and air conditioning—is attached to the H3's interior firewall. Neil Johnson

The Shreveport line is designed to enhance the ergonomics of vehicle assembly. The skillets can lift the H3 to the proper position so parts can be installed without too much lifting or bending by workers. Neil Johnson

wire cage to accept the skillet that carries the silver-colored shell that will become a HUMMER H3.

Most body panels for the H3 are stamped at Shreveport, with some pieces coming from GM's Marion (Indiana) and Parma (Ohio) Metal Centers. They are joined into the shape and structure of the H3—a body shell comprised of fenders, floor, doors, roof, and rear swing gate—by the more than 400 robotic welders in the Shreveport body shop.

At the first station on Trim Line 1, UAW members install the struts that hold the H3's hood open and also the rubber moldings around the door openings. The next stations install a variety of wiring harnesses, the rear window wiper motor, and the hood louvers.

About this time, workers remove the front doors and place them on a rack; the rear doors come off and go on another rack. The doors are painted along with the vehicle, but then are removed to ease installation of various interior components. Suddenly, the racks carrying the doors disappear, only to reappear much later in the assembly process when they are rejoined to their original vehicle. This is just one of many logistic miracles that occur in the assembly process.

Installation of the sunroof presents a challenge. Even with a moving mechanical arm doing the heave lifting, it isn't easy to get the glass and metal structure aligned quickly into the opening in the H3 roof. Like the installation of the large ceiling liner later on, maneuvering

Each station along the line has its own team of workers, who coordinate their movements much like a NASCAR pit crew. The team has only around 50 seconds to complete its work before the skillet takes the H3 to the next station. Neil Johnson

things into their proper place in the upper sections of the interior takes some experience and must be done more by feel than by sight.

Tonight, engineers help out, either physically or by jotting notes on clipboards or using cell phones to communicate with counterparts, whether on the other side of the assembly line or back in Michigan. But problems aren't commonplace, in large part because of the work already accomplished by the Front End Load Team (FELT), a group of hourly and waged employees from Shreveport that spent up to two years in Michigan helping to design and build H3 prototypes in preparation for the start of production.

The H3 scout takes a half an hour to make its way down Trim Line 1. At this point, its skillet goes back on

Work on interior components is easier with the doors removed. Neil Johnson

an elevator and up and over the plant floor to Trim Line 2, which leads it back toward the center of the X.

It is here that we notice how ergonomically friendly the Shreveport assembly line has been made. The bases around the skillets are wood and thus easier on legs and feet than the concrete factory floor. The skillets also rise and lower on cue so workers can install equipment with the least amount of bending and lifting. A UAW ergonomics observer explains that the equipment is adjusted shift by shift, accommodating a shorter worker on one shift and a taller one on the next.

Additional wiring harnesses, taillamps, the headliner, windshield wiper motors, heating and ventilation systems, and the instrument panel are installed, followed by a rear subwoofer for the audio system, the rear cargo mat, passenger compartment carpeting, and interior grab handles and other equipment before the H3 takes its next ride on the elevator and makes a right-hand turn to head down Trim Line 3.

It's 5:50 p.m. when the scout gets headlights, then seatbelts, then various interior panels. Trim pieces on the top of the vehicle are installed in a canyon-like area where workers stand on elevated platforms that put them in proper position for such things.

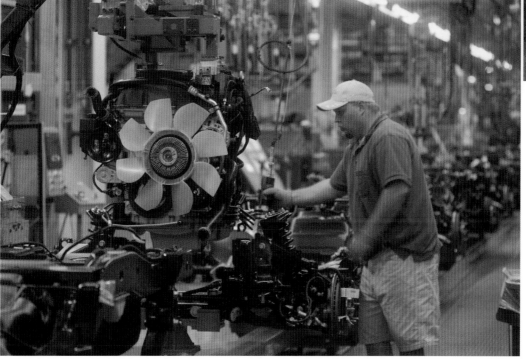

As the body shell makes its way through the four trim lines, the frame has been making its way through the chassis area. Near the end of its trip, its engine is dropped into place. **Neil Johnson**

After completing all four trim lines, the H3 body moves into position for its "marriage" to its frame and powertrain. Neil Johnson

The marriage ceremony completed, an H3 rides the conveyor down to the final assembly line. **Neil Johnson**

Shortly after 6:00 p.m., the H3 scout reaches the end of Trim Line 3, where robots install heavy glass panels, including the windshield.

Another elevator ride takes the scout to the head of Trim Line 4, where it gets the H3 badge on its rear swing gate and the cowl grille, windshield wipers, steering column, and ignition key are installed.

The body shell reaches the end of this line just in time for a 20-minute break. When work resumes, the scout will be first in line to get back on an elevator for the turn that takes it to the start of the Chassis Line, where the H3 body will be "married" to its frame.

WHILE THE BODY HAS BEEN WORKING ITS WAY ALONG THE VARIOUS TRIM LINES, a frame has been moving around the chassis arm of the Shreveport X. Much of this time, the frame has been inverted to ease

Fenders, placed in sequence to match the color of the vehicle coming down the final assembly line, await installation. **Neil Johnson**

component installation. Differentials, half shafts, suspension control arms, the fuel tank, and other parts are bolted to the frame, which gets its engine and transmission just before making its way to its union with an H3 body.

The marriage—and yes, that's really what they call it—looks like the mating ritual you see on television's nature channels. The chassis is below and ahead of the body, which has been released from its skillet and moves now by an overhead holder. The body catches up to the chassis and actually moves slightly ahead before the chassis slides in underneath.

The marriage is consummated by robotic equipment that secures the dozen bolts that join body and chassis into a single vehicle that is carried again by a skillet, which now climbs the conveyor system and winds its way to the fourth axis of Shreveport's X: Final Assembly.

It's 8:15 p.m. as the H3 scout gets underhood wiring harnesses, has its brake lines checked, its battery installed, and its flared fenders bolted on. The spare tire holder and spare tire are installed on the rear swing gate. While this goes on at the rear of the car, the center console is installed and the on-board computers are connected.

A mechanical arm carries the weight as a rear seat is moved into position. **Neil Johnson**

The rear seat goes in, then the front passenger's seat, and finally the driver's seat. The final line then makes a detour to the station where fluids are filled.

After that, it's back to the line for inner fenders, rocker panels, and tires, which work their way down one of two cyclone-shaped troughs. By now it's 9:15 p.m. and time for a 30-minute dinner break.

The line resumes at 9:48 p.m. with the H3 scout vehicle taking its final ride on an elevator and the last leg of final assembly. Standing on end, the H3 grille is 6 feet

tall, and getting it mounted properly on the front of the scout vehicle involves team members and engineers; there will be meetings later to talk about adjustments in the process.

Air bag drivers are installed. Gasoline goes into the fuel tank. Like magic, the hangers with the doors reappear as the vehicle leaves the gas station, and the doors are reattached.

The sections of the rear fender that extend over the rear doors are attached. From a trough beneath the line,

Halfway through final assembly, the H3 moves into an alcove near the line for the filling of most of its fluids. Gasoline will be added later in another station. **Neil Johnson**

the skid plate and other underbody components are installed. The HUMMER insignia goes on the sides of the vehicle, followed by the wheel hub covers, the air boxes, and the Monroney sticker—with its list of standard and optional equipment, and pricing and fuel economy information—is placed on the window.

Like the fuel filling area, this part of the line has special ventilation because the engine is started and allowed to warm up. Transmission fluid is topped off and the engine computer is set.

The H3 goes through a tunnel of bright lights where inspectors go over the vehicle inch by inch.

Wheels and tires make their way down a cyclone-shaped silo and are lifted with a mechanical arm into position, then bolted into place. **Neil Johnson**

Finally, at 10:45 p.m., the H3 is driven off the line. But Shreveport isn't done with it yet.

The H3 scout is driven to an area inside the assembly plant adjacent to the final line for dynamic testing. Wheel alignment, headlamp aim, and steering and suspension are verified before the car is driven a short distance to a dynamic vehicle test (DVT) chamber, where the H3 wheels ride on the rollers of a chassis dynamometer at speeds in excess of 60 miles per hour.

Then the vehicle is driven into a stall where water under high pressure is used to confirm there are no leaks in the bodywork or windows.

After yet another inspection under bright lights, the scout is certified as a genuine HUMMER H3 and driven out the factory's big garage doors and into the moonlit Louisiana night.

Standing on end, the H3's grille is as tall as someone 6 feet in height. **Neil Johnson**

The grille in place, the H3 heads down the final leg of final assembly, ready for inspection and a brief test drive. Neil Johnson

Chapter 6

Rock 'n' Roll

Putting the H3 Through Its Paces

"The Corvette will do 186 miles per hour, but maybe only one percent of the car's owners will ever drive that fast. Not many H3 owners will ever do the Rubicon."

—*Todd Hubbard, H3 vehicle dynamics engineer*

An H3 prototype splashes through a tomato soup-colored puddle on the Soldier Pass trail through red rock country in Sedona, Arizona. **Brenda Priddy & Company**

Maybe Smiley Rock was smiling because it knew something we didn't know. Maybe its benign "Happy Face" was really a sly grin, a "heh-heh-heh" born of the knowledge of how difficult its relatives just up the trail were going to make the next leg of our journey.

Todd Hubbard, vehicle dynamics engineer, has brought a HUMMER H3 "integration prototype," complete with his hand-painted switchgear indicators, to General Motors' Desert Proving Grounds (DPG) in Mesa, Arizona. There, he set up base camp to scout roads and trails that might be used for the H3's official introduction to the automotive press.

Hubbard's production-intent H3 prototype has the "Adventure" package, which is what HUMMER calls the H3 off-road option. This prototype has 33-inch Bridgestone all-terrain tires, a variety of under-vehicle skid plates, and a rear locking differential. However, it does not have the 4.03:1 rock-crawler reduction gear, but rather the standard 2.61 rear axle.

As Hubbard drives north out of Phoenix, he is joined by John Chapman and David Williams of the DPG technical staff, who bring along a HUMMER H2 as a support vehicle for the reconnoiter of such aptly named Arizona off-road trails as Greasy Spoon, Broken Arrow, Soldier Pass, Backway to Crown King, and Smiley Rock.

Four-wheel guidebooks rate these trails between 5 and 7 on the off-road difficulty scale. In general terms, a 5 requires a robust vehicle and "may be impassable for inexperienced drivers." On a trail rated 7, you better be not only experienced, but truly skilled at off-road driving because "these trails include very challenging sections with extremely steep grades, loose surfaces, large rocks, deep ruts, and/or tight clearances"—the books also recommend that you have a winch handy, just in case.

Photographer Brenda Priddy and I are along to enjoy such "fun."

———

THE SMILEY ROCK TRAIL WINDS OUT OF JEROME, ARIZONA, A HISTORIC mining town perched on the side of Cleopatra Hill, which affords a spectacular view across the greenery of the Verde Valley to the red rocks of Sedona and beyond to the snow-covered majesty of Humphreys Peak—at 12,643 feet, the tallest mountain in Arizona. Smiley the rock is located 17.7 miles into the 23.3-mile trail that bears its name. The first 15 of those miles are comprised of mainly shelf road that clings to the edge of Woodchute Mountain. But once you cross a small meadow, the degree of difficulty suddenly takes an extreme escalation. It is time to engage the "4Low" locked setting for the H3's transfer case.

At first, it's just that the trail narrows and gets rough and rocky, though it's hard not to smile back at Smiley Rock, which sits just to the left of the primitive path about midway through Martin Canyon. However, just beyond the smiling edifice the trail seems to disappear. Instead of something you might consider to be a drivable "trail," you're confronted with a narrow wash filled with boulders of varying sizes, ranging from a foot in diameter to those about the size and shape of a Volkswagen Beetle.

I'm sure that we've missed a turn somewhere, because there's no way this vehicle or anything that hasn't undergone extensive modification after leaving the factory is going to find a way up and over and through this boulder field. But Hubbard's guidebook and the trail map he downloaded into the global positioning satellite

The H3 is the most nimble member of the HUMMER family.

The H3 prototype leads the way along Smiley Rock trail, which soon will seem to disappear into a wash full of big boulders. Even with a vehicle as capable as the H3, it's always best to travel with at least two vehicles when doing severe off-roading, so we brought along a trail-tested H2 from GM's Desert Proving Ground. Larry Edsall

The H3 prototype made easy work of a serious and slippery climb up Sedona's red rock. Brenda Priddy & Company

The stair master: H3 prototype goes where other SUVs fear to tread, and in the case of these steep and slick red rock "stairs," it got there without needing to engage its rear axle locker. **Brenda Priddy & Company**

receiver taped to the top of the dashboard say this is indeed the trail.

Hubbard reaches over from the passenger's seat to engage the button on which he's painted a I–X–I symbol, indicating the H3's locking rear differential, which provides for maximum traction. We take a deep breath and inch forward very carefully, as though we're entering a minefield.

The beneath-the-body apron, rocker-panel protection rails, and other under-vehicle armor take a beating. We get high-centered a couple of times, but Hubbard says to just back up and try another line, or to turn the steering wheel back and forth, using the high-centered spot as a pivot point until the traction system helps the tires regain grip. Finally, though, he gets out to serve as a spotter so I can line up the H3's big front tires with boulders, taking advantage of the H3's 39.4-degree angle of approach to use the rocks as stepping stones. Meanwhile, I'm hoping the H2 that's following us will be able to make it far enough through the rocks to winch us out when we get stuck.

Except we don't get stuck. We bang and whack and bounce—somehow bending the bottom edge of the rear license plate but not damaging any of the vehicle's sheet metal. And somehow, the H3's powertrain and the technology that keeps its wheels fighting for traction-even on boulders slick from recent rains and the snow that falls while we're on the trail—keep us going.

Hubbard says this stretch of Smiley Rock is just like the Rubicon Trail, except the Rubicon goes on for more than 12 miles and thus takes two days to complete. Sure,

Pretty dirty: With three layers of material even in their sidewalls, Bridgestone's 33-inch off-road tires may get dirty, but they hold up to the rigors of extreme rock crawling. **Brenda Priddy & Company**

you could walk it faster than you can drive it, but it's the driving that makes it so much fun.

GETTING THROUGH THAT BOULDER-FILLED WASH CREATES SATISFIED SMILES even wider than Smiley Rock's.

Hubbard says having the capability right from the factory to handle trails such as Smiley Rock and the Rubicon helps establish the H3's credentials.

"It's like the Corvette," he explains. "The Corvette will do 186 miles per hour, but maybe only one percent of the car's owners will ever drive that fast. Not many H3 owners will ever do the Rubicon."

But they could if they chose to.

Among the things that make the H3 so good off-road are the obvious—ground clearance, approach and departure and break-over angles, 33-inch tires with three-ply sidewalls to protect from punctures, and the gearing and traction systems. But there also are technologies that aren't so obvious—at least not until you really need them—things such as low-gear throttle progression and transmission shift-point adjustment, secondary front jounce bumpers, and even the vehicle's roll center geometry.

"When you're in low range, you get a different [computer] mapping for the throttle progression," Hubbard explains. "It's a speed-based progression and it's the first of its type for General Motors. Basically, it turns the gain down so that when you're trying to be precise and in control [such as when stepping over boulders], your foot, for a given amount of pedal travel,

The road may not be pavement smooth, but those inside the H3 remain comfortable as the vehicle's suspension and body geometry are designed to absorb the worst of the rough stuff. **Brenda Priddy & Company**

Sedona's red rock formations provide a beautiful backdrop for the H3. **Brenda Priddy & Company**

Even with its wide stance, the mid-size H3 has room to maneuver when the trail narrows. Its nimble 37-foot turning circle enhances the vehicle's dexterity. **Brenda Priddy & Company**

doesn't get as much throttle response. What it allows you to do is to be a lot smoother so you're not bouncing your foot in and out of the throttle. It helps both ascending and descending."

The system engages only when the H3 is shifted into low gear, and it affects not only the throttle but also the shift points for the automatic transmission.

"The one-two shift is pushed out," Hubbard explains. "A lot of times, when you're crawling, you want to get a little higher rpm to generate some higher torque, but you don't want to command [force] that one-two shift.

"Because we have such a numerically high crawl ratio, when you do get that one-two shift, the pressures are greatly reduced so it's not so snappy. It's nothing you'd want on the road, but again, this is just in the 4Low calibration."

The H3 dynamics team worked hard on all aspects of the vehicle's suspension. The team did high-speed tuning in the desert near Barstow, California, where it kept bending shock absorber rods until it switched from 11-millimeter units to 14-millimeter rods like those in the H2—another example of making whatever changes were required to make the H3 a genuine HUMMER.

"We haven't bent a shock rod since," says Hubbard. He adds that the team worked closely with shock supplier, Tenneco Automotive, and brake system supplier, ADVICS, to enhance both off-road traction and on-road control.

"We were on Cadillac Hill [one of the most challenging parts of the Rubicon Trail] and it was raining and really slippery and the traction control system worked superbly," he says.

"At the Desert Proving Grounds is what they officially call a 'strike through' bump," he says. "We call it the 'stupid' bump. At sixty to sixty-five miles per hour, I can fly this vehicle forty feet at two to three feet off the ground and it stays level and it doesn't crash down when it lands."

I ask Hubbard why, even when we were crawling over the minefield of boulders in Martin Canyon, we weren't getting the severe head toss experienced in even less extreme environments in other SUVs. In answer, he talks about how the lower spring rates, designed to enhance on-road ride, also absorb more of the off-road terrain. He discusses suspension geometry, especially in the rear, where the H3 has a Hotchkiss setup with multi-leaf springs. He talks about roll stiffness, damping and the "roll center axis," determined by the H3's suspension

Treading lightly: The H3 leaves barely a ripple as it makes its way along an off-road trail. **Brenda Priddy & Company**

geometry, and the H3's center of gravity, determined by the vehicle's overall mass, and how their relationship helps to keep things calm in the cabin when the suspension appears to be fighting for its life.

———————

"WE BELIEVE THAT THE H3 IS EVERY BIT AS CAPABLE OFF-ROAD AS THE H2," says Lori Cumming, General Motors chief engineer for small and midsize trucks. "[At] every step of the development we kept in mind that we

absolutely had to have best off-road performance."

But, she adds, "I can't wait for people to get the opportunity to drive it on-road."

At least 80 percent of H3 vehicle dynamics development involved on-pavement performance. While the H3 had to be the best off-road in its class, the team knew that H3 owners will spend most of their time on pavement, driving back and forth to work, taking children to and from school, sports activities, shopping, religious services, running errands, even pulling a boat to the lake

Vehicle performance manager Kevin Dinger rides along to answer questions (and to make sure I don't wreak havoc in one of only a handful of finished HUMMERs the factory has produced at this point). Somewhere in metro Detroit, H3 Product Manager Michele Mack is fretting with motherly concern about letting one of her babies not only out of her sight, but out of her control. We promise to be careful.

We pick up the H3 at General Motors' main proving grounds and head to nearby Milford, Michigan, where I want to see how easy—or how difficult—it is to do a parallel parking maneuver and to see if the upright windshield made it difficult to see overhead traffic signals.

DRIVING THE H3 GIVES YOU THE SECURE FEELING OF BEING IN a mobile turret or rolling fortress. Although the step up isn't at all severe, the ratio of sheet metal to glass on the H3's flanks makes its side windows appear almost like slits rather than glass expanses. Still, I have no difficulty seeing what is going on around the vehicle. And the upright windshield does not hide overhead stoplights.

Parallel parking is no chore at all. The H3 has a wheelbase that's nearly half a foot shorter than a Chevrolet Malibu Maxx. Even with its rear-mounted spare tire, the H3 is more than an inch shorter overall than the compact wagon. With a 37-foot turning radius, the H3 also is more maneuverable, even when wearing these big all-terrain tires.

The HUMMER H1 can be ungainly in town and the H2 can be cumbersome, but the H3 feels nimble, even agile.

Convinced that the H3 can handle parking stripes on concrete as well as it does a boulder-floored wash, we leave Milford's quaint downtown and head toward Interstate 96 to see how the H3 responds in high-speed traffic.

I put the pedal to the metal on the on ramp and the 3.5-liter inline five-cylinder engine doesn't hesitate. In fact, the Vortec powerplant emits a nice powerful sound as the H3 accelerates and then quiets quite properly

Turret-like windows enhance the feeling of security while riding in the H3, yet the driver and passengers still have good visibility in all directions.

While striving to be "best off-road," engineers didn't forget the fact that most people will do most of their driving on pavement, where the H3 is smooth but still sure-footed.

or snowmobiles to the country, and, hopefully, taking an occasional off-road adventure.

My on-road adventure with the H3 is in one of the first "non-saleable" units built at the Shreveport factory. Like the prototype I drove on the Smiley Rock trail, this H3 is equipped with 33-inch tires and an automatic transmission. But it also has full factory sheet metal, painted Victory Red, and a finished interior trimmed out in light cashmere with ebony piping and equipped with a huge, sliding-glass sunroof.

The H3 provides serenity in the sometimes daunting urban environment.

when we reach cruising speed. That doesn't take very long at all. Soon we're zipping along at 70 miles per hour, perhaps even a little faster considering the flow of traffic in the Detroit area.

Even with what appears to be the aerodynamics of a couple of bricks, there is very little wind and no tire noise or axle whine coming into the H3's cabin. Dinger and I carry on our conversation in normal speaking tones. The engineering and design teams worked closely and worked hard on such things as wind tunnel tuning of the radiuses of the sheet metal around the upright windshield and the air boxes near the base of the windshield pillars. The result was enhanced aerodynamics, and by several points, and the return on investment was not just a quieter cabin, but up to 20 miles per gallon in fuel economy on the highway.

The engineering staff in Michigan also praises the Shreveport factory and its hourly United Auto Workers employees for the way they have come up with new ways

H3 has the look and capabilities of a HUMMER, but combines them in a right-sized package.

to install door seals to limit wind noise caused by the iconic H3 design, which puts the seam where door meets roofline in the direct airflow rather than tucked away.

The H3 absorbs the imperfections of Michigan's rough roads just as nicely as it deals with big off-road boulders. There's not hint of bump steer or unwelcome feedback through the very thick rim of the steering wheel. Steering is nicely weighted and responsive, with good on-center feel.

Brake pedal feel also is good and the brake system responds quickly and surely when I ask it to slow or stop us. I noticed while off-roading that the threshold between slowing and stopping while rock crawling can be tricky to find at first, though once you educate your foot, the brakes respond very well to pedal pressure nuances.

Cruising along the Interstate, I can easily find switchgear controls, now factory finished rather than hand painted and large enough to be manipulated even by gloved hands. I also notice the extenders built into the sun visors, a very useful feature in the Sun Belt.

Gauges are easy to read. Dinger notes that one late change made just before production was to enhance the driver's view of the gauge cluster and driver information center display so they could be read more easily in bright sunlight.

The leather-covered seats not only look sharp with their contrast-colored piping, but they are comfortable and supportive, nicely but not overly bolstered, and with good lumbar support. The headrest is close to the back of your head, properly positioned to provide protection if someone smacks you from behind.

Getting hit from behind seems a possibility today. The weather is quickly deteriorating. The day before our drive, dozens of cars were involved in a weather-related chain collision on this same highway. In just the last few minutes the temperature has dropped nearly 20 degrees. What were sprinkles have turned into icy, snowy precipitation.

But the H3 remains surefooted, even as we hustle through the arc of the ramp that leads us off the Interstate and onto U.S. 23 to begin working our way back toward the Milford Proving Grounds.

There's room to spare when the H3 pulls into a parking spot, even when maneuvering into a parallel space.

BEFORE HANDING OVER THE KEYS TO ONE OF HER VEHICLES, Michele Mack had told me that I'd find "nothing watered-down, nothing rebadged."

She's right. Nothing about the H3 even whispers of its early development ties to the Colorado and Canyon, even though those are surprisingly capable vehicles in their own right.

The H3's heritage is H1 and H2. It earns its HUMMER badge.

Chapter 7

The Road (and Off-Road) Ahead

H4 and More

"'We could do this,' and, 'We could do this.'"

—*Clay Dean, GM director of vehicle design*

The H3 shows that a HUMMER can be brawny without being too big, and thus opens the brand to a variety of future models.

H1. H2. H3. So what's next for HUMMER? An H3 SUT seems certain. Not one like the little H3T pickup truck concept, but a version of the H3 SUV with a pickup truck bed instead of a hard-covered cargo area—something much like the "open-top" version of the H1 or the H2 SUT.

Expect an H4, an H5, and maybe even an H6, though as the numbers increase, so does the likelihood that the vehicle architecture will deviate from SUV to pickup truck to perhaps even an all-terrain vehicle or personal watercraft.

Whether future HUMMERs have four wheels, or two, or three, or snowmobile tracks, or water jets, two criteria will remain: HUMMERs will have iconic design. HUMMERs will have exceptional off-pavement capabilities. Just imagine a HUMMER jet ski with paramilitary styling cues and the capability to climb Class V rapids . . . .

"It's pretty exciting to take a brand like HUMMER and lay it out and say, 'We could do this,' and, 'We could do this,'" says Clay Dean, who was doing just that in his design studio before being promoted to director of vehicle design for General Motors' future midsize cars.

HUMMER brand product director Marc Hernandez says the team has laid out a strategy that will explore utilities of all sizes, pickup trucks of all sizes, and nontraditional vehicles.

The team's experimentation was not limited to vehicle formats or off-road prowess. Something responsive to California's and other states' air quality and fuel efficiency concerns is also in the works. The hydrogen-powered H2H driven by HUMMER patron and California governor Arnold Schwarzenegger is something the HUMMER team was talking about as early as 1999.

Although the original military Humvee was big because it needed to be, large size is not an essential HUMMER attribute. The company is exploring designs for machines that are much smaller, lighter, more nimble, and more efficient. One such project, called H.5 ("H point five"), is in development with Brigham Young University, Kettering University, and Virginia Tech.

"H.5 reinvents the off-road category," says Dean. "Say you have a HUMMER that's constructed more like a motorcycle. It's very lightweight, maybe a 1200-cc motor and it carries two people, maybe three, and maybe there's a diesel or a hybrid involved."

Actor Dennis Quaid enjoys the view of the HUMMER Fashion Show held during the annual Jiffy Lube Dennis Quaid Charity Classic golf tournament in Austin, Texas.

The H.5 could cruise city streets, but wouldn't be meant for freeway traffic. But because of its size and light weight, it would have off-road capability beyond even any other HUMMER, yet could be priced at less than $20,000. Not only might it reinvent the category, it could reinvent what people think of HUMMER. With its lightweight and clean powertrain, it would leave virtually no impact on the environment.

"We call it the green HUMMER," says Dean. "It's a vehicle for search and rescue, the forest service, beaches, lifeguards. It gives you one more step in implementing the idea that HUMMER is a vehicle for all people to do all sorts of things."

"We have to strategically think about entering and exiting segments," adds Marc Hernandez.

"One of the things that manufacturers have a tendency to do, because of emotion, because of whatever, we tend to stay too long at the party," says Marc Hernandez. "You have to look at your portfolio and say, 'Does it make sense for this one to stay here?'

Just days before winning the Academy Award as the best actor for 2005, Jamie Foxx took the stage with the HUMMER H3 in the annual GM "ten" fashion show, which pairs celebrities, fashions, and the hottest General Motors vehicles in a charity fundraiser in Los Angeles. The event raised more than $100,000 for P.S. Arts, an organization striving to restore arts education to public schools.

As governor of California, Arnold Schwarzenegger called for the establishment of the "Hydrogen Highway," where what many consider the automotive fuel of the future would be readily available. GM built the HUMMER H2H to support that initiative. The H2H is equipped with a supercharged, 6.0-liter Vortec 6000 V-8 engine that burns hydrogen fuel instead of gasoline. Instead of hydrocarbons and other pollutants, hot water is emitted from its tailpipe.

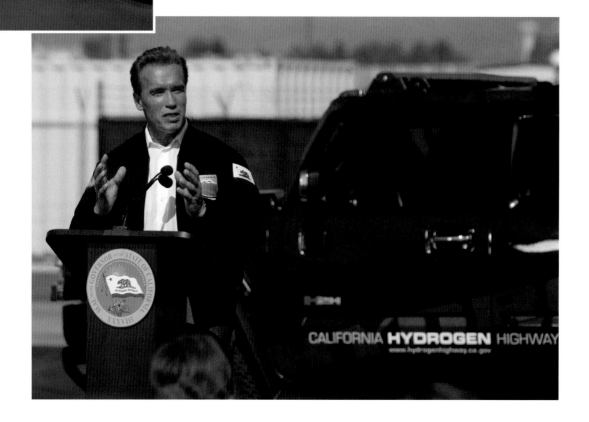

An H2 yanks an abandoned vehicle out of a wilderness area as part of HUMMER Helps, a program in conjunction with Tread Lightly!'s Restoration for Recreation that promotes socially responsible four-wheeling through the enhancement of recreational areas.

The HUMMER H1 and even the H2 may have been considered toys for big boys (and girls), but HUMMERs are available in all sizes, including this Little Tikes HUMMER ride-on vehicle.

Even the HUMMER Tactical mountain bike comes with a military heritage. The folding system was developed so paratroopers could make a quick exit from aircraft with a full-sized bicycle. The bicycles fit in a pack that is 3 square feet and only 1 foot deep.

"Let's look at the SUT, for example. If we enter the pickup truck arena, if we do a full-size pickup, do we keep the (H2) SUT? Those are the decisions we have to make."

Ironically, the SUT was not in HUMMER's original product plans. Sometimes an automaker will launch a new model—one not so far from existing production—to generate excitement. This is what happened with the H2 SUT. HUMMER's first general manager, Mike DiGiovanni, needed a bridge between the H2 and H3 to justify dealers' investment and maintain consumer interest.

The H2 made its debut as a 2002 model. Sales took off like a rocket ship. Some 18 months later they had settled into orbit, so the H2 SUT was introduced for the 2004 model year. The H2 SUT freshened the brand and kept it going strong until the H3's debut.

But what follows H3? Look for H3 SUT. Perhaps H3 SC—as in supercharged. Also look for H3 overseas.

"We're getting ready to grow rather significantly outside of the United States," says Susan Docherty, who succeeded DiGiovanni as HUMMER general manger in the summer of 2004.

Some 10 percent of H2 production is exported out of North America, primarily to Europe and the Middle East.

"We now have a product from a size, fuel-efficiency, and packaging standpoint that's appropriate for international markets," says Docherty. "We're going to be letting the newest member, and the smaller sibling, out to places and to people who are experiencing the brand for the very first time."

Docherty sees global potential for the brand and wants the flexibility to be able to build a smaller HUMMER for sale in particular markets, such as Asia. But she also knows that there are things that HUMMER cannot, and will not, be.

"We know it's not a minivan and it's not a small car," she says, adding that a HUMMER can never be a soft-road vehicle; it must always be the most capable in its class off-road.

"But there is some territory within the industry in which this brand could expand," Docherty says. "Our H3T concept vehicle, that's a perfect example of a segment you could go to where iconic design and unparalleled off-road capability are needed."

HUMMER may also expand to the most paved places on the planet. Clay Dean says the HUMMER team was surprised by the H2's acceptance by people who bought it for the street rather than for off-roading.

"When they bought them and starting putting 24-inch wheels and everything on them, we never in our wildest imaginations thought they would do that," Dean says. However, he adds, "Our initial sketches of

Continued on page 141

Just as a sport utility truck (SUT) version of the H2 followed the H2 SUV into production, an H3 SUT likely will be the next vehicle to join the HUMMER lineup.

Wisconsin HUMMER dealer John Bergstrom was the first to open a new Quonset-hut-style dealership.

A ceiling fan with blades so long they resemble those of a helicopter allows dealers to give the impression that the HUMMERs on display were airlifted in by the military.

Each HUMMER dealership includes a vehicle capabilities demonstration area with a variety of obstacles that showcase the HUMMER's unique qualities.

"Alpha" is the name selected for the higher-performance versions of HUMMER vehicles. The first to launch was the 2006 HUMMER H1, powered by a 6.6-liter diesel engine that delivers 300 horsepower, a 46 percent increase over the standard H1. An H2 Alpha and H3 Alpha figure to be in the pipeline.

The HUMMER H3T concept vehicle was powered by a turbocharged version of the H3's inline five-cylinder Vortec 3500 engine. A power-boosting supercharger likely will be used to increase output for an H3 Alpha model.

In the summer of 2004, Susan Docherty succeeded Mike DiGiovanni as only the second general manager in HUMMER history. Docherty, who had been at Cadillac, calls herself the "steward" of the brand, both for its continued development in North America and also for its expansion to overseas markets.

HUMMER general manager Susan Docherty displays an American Red Cross HUMMER as part of a program in which members of the HUMMER Club Inc. can become certified as Red Cross volunteers using their vehicles in a coordinated disaster relief effort to drive people and supplies into areas other vehicles might not be able to reach. The program's official name is HOPE—HUMMER Owners Prepared for Emergencies.

HUMMER Hr

Hr, a small, light weight HUMMER for diverse LA environs and events...
Mulholland Drive and Latigo Canyon, riots and earthquakes,
PCH, The Rock Store and Crystal Cove,
stuck on the 4 level or lunch at the Polo Lounge.

Hr is an indestructible piece of urban jewelry,
crafted from methods and materials
which cannot be mass produced...
a techno rat rod.

Hr is consistent with HUMMER brand cues
and emotive positioning.

Hr challenges and redefines traditional
HUMMER perception.

GLAMS.

QUAKES.

CARVES.

SIGS.

COASTS.

AND DOES LA.
LIKE NOTHING ELSE

Los Angeles is the epicenter of American car culture and home to the Art Center College of Design where many car designers are educated and the advanced design studios where many of them work. To celebrate this unique design space, the Los Angeles International Auto Show in 2005 hosted a competition. Automakers' West Coast studios were asked to submit their ideas for the "ultimate" L.A. vehicle. The Hr, short for HUMMER roadster, was the entry from 5350 Industrial Concepts, the General Motors design studio in West Hollywood.

With wheels pushed to the corners and unparalleled off-road capabilities on the beach and in the California canyons, Hr shows that a HUMMER doesn't have to look like a truck or sport utility vehicle.

Continued from page 135

HUMMER had almost that same appearance. But we never thought it would be embraced as aggressively on the street as it is. We learned from that, learned from the customers. There are two different categories (on-pavement and off) that have yet to be really explored. As a designer, you want these challenges. We have more ideas than we have opportunities to present them."

One idea that GM's west coast design studio presented at the 2005 Los Angeles Auto Show was the Hr, the HUMMER roadster. Los Angeles is home to the world's most important automotive design school, Art Center College of Design, and more than a dozen major automaker design studios. The Los Angeles Auto Show staged a competition among the studios to create the "ultimate L.A. machine."

The entry from GM's 5350 Industrial Concepts studio in West Hollywood was a small, lightweight HUMMER "for diverse L.A. environs and events . . . Mulholland Drive and Latigo Canyon, riots and

earthquakes, Pacific Coast Highway, The Rock Store, and Crystal Cove. Hr is an indestructible piece of urban jewelry, crafted from methods and materials which cannot be mass produced. . . ."

Dean sees GM using HUMMER as a halo brand for four-wheel drive just as it uses the Corvette for the development of high-performance powertrains that trickle down to other vehicles.

"Now that H3 is here, there are several doors we can go through next and they're all pretty exciting," Dean promises. "I think every year or two you'll see a concept to reinforce where we want to go. . . ."

And where is that?

"H1 competed not with another car," says Dean, "but with a home or yacht or helicopter. It was very much a luxury purchase. The buyer didn't need it. He wanted it. You have to keep that in mind.

"HUMMER is not a vehicle you need. HUMMER is a vehicle you want. HUMMER has more than what's necessary. We don't want to lose that."

Looking capable isn't enough. The HUMMER H3 delivers on its visual promise with its go-anywhere capabilities.

	2005 H1	2005 H2	2006 H3
Ground clearance	16 inches	9.7 inches	9.1 inches
Approach angle	72 degrees	40.8 degrees	39.4 degrees with 33-inch tires 37.5 degrees with 32-inch tires
Departure angle	37.5 degrees	39.6 degrees	36.5 degrees with 33-inch tires 35.5 degrees with 32-inch tires
Breakover angle	32.5 degrees	25.8 degrees	25 degrees with 33-inch tires 24 degrees with 32-inch tires
Water fording	30 inches	20 inches	24 inches at 5 miles per hour 16 inches at 20 miles per hour
Grade capability (percent)	60 (31 degrees)	60	60
Side slope capability (degree)	40 (22 degrees)	40	40
Wheelbase	130 inches	122.8 inches	111.9 inches
Length	184.5 inches	203.5 inches	186.7 inches (includes spare tire)
Width	101 inches	81.2 inches	74.7 inches
Height	75 inches	78.5 inches	74.5 inches
Track (front)	71.6 inches	69.4 inches	65 inches
Track (rear)	71.6 inches	69.4 inches	65.5 inches
Curb weight	7558 pounds	6400 pounds	4700 pounds (with automatic transmission)
Towing capacity	7409 pounds	6700 pounds	4500 pounds
Engine	6.5-liter V-8 diesel	6.0-liter V-8	3.5-liter inline five-cylinder
Horsepower	205 at 3,200 rpm	325 at 5,200 rpm	220 at 5,600 rpm
Torque	440 at 1,800 rpm	365 ft-lb at 4,000 rpm	225 ft-lb at 2,800 rpm
Transmission	four-speed automatic	four-speed automatic	five-speed manual or four-speed automatic
Final drive	4.91	4.10	4.10 (manual), 4.56 (automatic)
Low-range gear reduction	1.92	2.64	2.64 (manual), 4.03 (automatic)
Crawl ratio (range)	41.5:1	33:01:00	33-69:1 (manual or automatic)
Recommended fuel	No. 2 diesel	87 octane	87 octane
Fuel tank	25 gallons	32 gallons	23 gallons
Fuel economy	10–11 miles per gallon (est.)	12–13 miles per gallon (est.)	16 city, 20 highway (manual) 16 city, 19 highway (automatic)
Chassis	full-size body-on-frame heavy-duty sport utility vehicle	full-size body-on-frame sport utility vehicle	midsize body-on-frame sport utility vehicle
Front suspension	independent double A-frame, 27-millimeter stabilizer bar	independent with torsion bars, 46-millimeter monotube gas shocks, 36-millimeter stabilizer bar	independent short/long arm torsion bar, 46-millimeter monotube gas-charged shocks, 36-millimeter tubular stabilizer bar
Rear suspension	independent double A-frame	five-link with variable-rate coil spring (optional air springs), 46-millimeter monotube gas shocks, 30-millimeter stabilizer bar	Hotchkiss design multileaf, semi-elliptical single-stage leaf springs, 46-millimeter monotube gas-charged shocks, 25-millimeter rear solid diameter stabilizer bar
Steering	power-assisted recirculating ball	power-assisted variable-ratio recirculating ball	power-assisted rack-and-pinion with tri-bushing mount
Steering ratio	13-16:1	variable 15-13:1	17-1
Lock-to-lock	2.5	3	3.25
Turning circle	26.5 feet	43.5 feet	37 feet
Brakes (front/rear)	10.5x0.94/10.5x0.94-inch discs (mounted inboard)	12.8x1.5/13.0x1.1-inch discs	12.4x1.1/12.3x0.5-inch discs
Wheels	17x8.5-inch high-strength	17x8 inches	16x7.5 inches
Tires	37X12.50 Goodyear with Central Tire Inflation System	LT315/70R17 all-terrain	P265/75R16 Goodyear all-terrain or LT285/75R16C Bridgestone on-/off-road
Seating	four	five	five
Front head/shoulder/hip/leg room	41.5/77.0/23.1/38.0 inches	40.5/66.4/62.9/41.3 inches	40.6/54.4/53.9/41.9 inches
Rear head/shoulder/hip/leg room	40.0/77.0/22.4/29.8 inches	39.7/66.3/62.0/38.6 in.	39.9/53.5/53.5/35 in.
3rd row head/shoulder/hip/leg room	not applicable	38.8/41.4/30.3/27.3 inches	not applicable
Cargo capacity	58.3 cubic feet	80.6 cubic feet with second and third rows down)	55.7 cubic feet (second row down) 29.5 cubic feet (second row up)
GVWR	12,100 pounds	8,600 pounds	5,850 pounds
Payload	2,742 pounds	2,000 pounds	1,150 pounds

Bibliography

Books

Bailey, L. Scott (publisher). *The American Car Since 1775*
(by the editors of *Automobile Quarterly*). New York:
Automobile Quarterly Inc., 1971.

Kimes, Beverly Rae and Clark, Henry Austin Jr. *Standard
Catalog of American Cars, 1805–1942.* Iola, WI;
Krause Publications, 1996.

Lamm, John and DeLorenzo, Matt. *Hummer H2.* St. Paul,
MN: MBI Publishing Company, 2002.

Massey, Peter and Wilson, Jeanne. *Backcountry
Adventures Arizona.* Castle Rock, CO: Swagman
Publishing, 2001.

Padgett, Marty. *Hummer: How a Little Truck Company
Hit the Big Time, Thanks to Saddam,
Schwarzenegger, and GM.* St. Paul, MN: MBI
Publishing Company, 2004.

Wells, Charles A. *Guide to Arizona Backroads & 4-Wheel
Drive Trails.* Colorado Springs, CO: FunTreks, Inc.,
2001.

Periodicals

"Hummer's Here," *AutoWeek*, November 2, 1992.

Mandel, Dutch. "I'll Be Back: H2 Arrives in 2002,"
AutoWeek, January 17, 2000.

Pewe, Rick. "The New Hummer H2: Everything the
Hummer Is—and Everything the Hummer Isn't,"
Peterson's 4Wheel and Off-Road, November 2001.

Stoll, John D. "Hummer Taps Nike for H3T," *Automotive
News*, January 5, 2004.

Vaughn, Mark. "Best in the West: The New H2 Does
More Things and Does Them Better Than Anything
Else Out There, Especially Way Out There,"
AutoWeek, June 10, 2002.

Other Sources

www.4wheeloffroad.com

www.izoom.com

General Motors and AM General websites and press
materials

Index